T0326956

Migration in the Medieval Mediterranean

PAST IMPERFECT

See further
www.arc-humanities.org/our-series/pi

Migration in the Medieval Mediterranean

Sarah Davis-Secord

British Library Cataloguing in Publication Data
A catalogue record for this book is available from the British Library

ISBN (print) 9781641892667
e-ISBN (PDF) 9781641892674
e-ISBN (EPUB) 9781641892681

www.arc-humanities.org
Printed and bound in the UK (by CPI Group [UK] Ltd), USA (by Bookmasters), and elsewhere using print-on-demand technology.

Contents

Introduction

Humans have been on the move for as long as they have been human. From the earliest migrations of *homo sapiens* out of Africa, to the influx of Germanic tribes and Eurasian steppe peoples who crossed the borders of the Roman Empire from the fourth century CE, all the way to the millions of refugees from Africa and the Middle East seeking entry into the European Union today, repeated waves of multidirectional migration have impacted political, cultural, linguistic, economic, and environmental landscapes for millennia. Indeed, large-scale migration has been one of the most influential factors shaping human history, and it shows no signs of stopping. And this fact is especially true when considering the history of the Mediterranean Sea. Just as today the Mediterranean Sea is a conduit for refugees and migrants, so too in the Middle Ages was it the field across which large numbers of people travelled for pilgrimage, politics, or profit, relocated or were relocated against their will, and sought refuge, safety, and gain.

Modern science has confirmed the depth of migration's impact through DNA analysis—of both modern populations and ancient ones. Study of "aDNA" (ancient DNA) is a growing field within archaeology and history. For example, a series of broad-based genetic studies have shown that all modern human populations contain strains of genetic material from wide varieties of different ancient locations; relatedly, they have found that no population's genetic material indicates long-term stability or ethnic purity. In fact, outside of Indigenous Australians, all modern human populations are the genetic result of waves of migration and mixing: that is, historically speaking, migration—not population stability—has been the norm. In other words, the long history of population movements on both large and small scales means that there are no "pure" races or ethnicities.[1]

And while the movement of human populations has an ancient pedigree, it is also the case that from the very earliest phase of human settlement during the Neolithic period, there has been conflict between settled communities and migratory peoples. One of the earliest surviving written stories, *The Epic of Gilgamesh*, a poem from ancient Mesopotamia, records the fear with which city-dwellers faced the "wild man" of nomadic cultures. Likewise, many modern media representations of refugees and migrants into European and American spaces highlight the fears and concerns that their arrival might inspire; such fear often leads to opposition to immigration. Modern migration patterns see millions of people fleeing war, genocide, famine, and poverty in Latin America, Africa, and the Middle East coursing into the European Union and the United States, only to there be faced with racist hostility, bureaucratic obstructions, difficulty finding gainful employment, and continuing poverty.

None of this is to say that directionalities, patterns, or volumes of migration have been constant across the millennia, or that historical numbers of long-distance migrants are comparable to modern ones. There is no way to quantify premodern migrants, unlike contemporary ones who are being tracked by both governmental and non-governmental agencies. For instance, the UNHCR, a division of the UN tasked with protecting refugees, keeps precise and up-to-date counts of the people attempting to cross the Mediterranean into Europe via different points of entry.[2] Premodern migra-

---

1 https://www.sciencemag.org/news/2017/05/theres-no-such-thing-pure-european-or-anyone-else.

2 https://data2.unhcr.org/en/situations/mediterranean.

tions certainly did not include as many known individuals, but that fact does not make them less historically significant. And we know that the pace and volume of migration has intensified at various times in history. Some periods have featured massive population movements, while others have seen only a trickle.

The European Middle Ages (roughly 500–1500 CE) was a time of considerable movement and migration, despite the stereotyped image of the period as static, locally-bound, and ignorant of the wider world. For some historians, in fact, the medieval period began at the moment in which Germanic tribal groups moved into the Roman Empire and fundamentally changed it: these large-scale migrations resulted in the establishment of new political communities within Europe that would come to be understood as the foundation of modern political states. Similarly, in some ways of thinking, the "Middle Ages" ended because Turkish groups who had migrated westward from steppe regions conquered the Byzantine capital of Constantinople in 1453. In this one sense, then, migration may define the very boundaries of the Middle Ages as a period of study.

Just like the millions of modern refugees who cross the Mediterranean in small boats and rafts destined for Greece and southern Italy, seeking a better life within the borders of Europe, many medieval migrants relocated within and across the Mediterranean Sea. The Mediterranean has long been an arena for the movements of peoples, goods, ideas, and pathogens. Before the Roman Empire made the inland sea their own (calling it *mare nostrum*, or "our sea") by conquering all of the surrounding land territories, both Phoenicians and Greeks sailed long distances across the Mediterranean and founded colonies far from their motherlands. Both groups originated in the eastern Mediterranean region but sent out waves of ships filled with trade goods and people who settled regions across both northern and southern shores of the western Mediterranean. From the mid-third century BCE, the Romans began to conquer those settlements along with many others populated by various peoples.

As the Roman republic transformed into an empire, the entire Mediterranean world came under Rome's political and economic control, encompassing a wide variety of languages, religions, and ethnicities. Even at its earliest stages, the ancient community of Romans traced their ancestry back to migrants from the eastern Mediterranean: one story they told themselves about the foundation of their city involved a refugee who fled from his destroyed city in the Near East, bringing with him only his father, his son, a few friends, and his family gods. Aeneas' trip across the Mediterranean in order to establish the city of Rome was, in fact, quite similar to those of many medieval and modern migrants: marked by the deaths of beloved family members, disastrous shipwrecks, uncertainty about where they would end up, and fears about how they would manage life in a new land.

As the Roman Empire broke up into the various medieval states and communities that constituted early medieval Byzantium, the Islamicate world, and the petty states of Latin Europe, this tradition of human mobility was transformed but not halted. Some of the most defining events of the late antique and early medieval periods, in fact, were large scale migration events and population movements. The massive influxes of Germanic, Slavic, and other peoples into the Roman Empire (formerly called the "barbarian migrations") between the late fourth to seventh centuries are often credited with sparking the end of the empire's existence as a united whole (although that interpretation continues to be debated by historians). Likewise, the movements of Muslims—primarily ethnically Arab, Bedouin, and Amazigh (Berber)—into the Mediterranean Sea region were fundamentally transformative for the post-Roman eastern hemisphere. And, outside of these broad demographic alterations, which brought thousands of new settlers, rulers, and other migrants into the lands of Europe, North Africa, and the Levant, individuals moved homes for a wide variety of reasons across the Middle Ages. Some relocated temporarily, others permanently. Some moved by choice—seeking profitable employment, marriage, or a safer place to live—and others against their will, as enslaved people, exiles, or refugees.

This book profiles a number of such medieval migrants, providing a peek into their lives, their motivations for migration, and the struggles they faced in new lands. Just like in the contemporary world, the vast majority of medieval asylum-seekers and refugees leave little or no trace in the historical records, meaning that their life stories are difficult or impossible to recover. But unlike in the modern world, where video and photography capture the devastation on the faces of crowds of refugees or the tragic sights of hundreds of migrants drowning during shipwrecks, for most of the medieval period even the very existence of migrants and asylum-seekers can seem undetectable. This book seeks to recover glimpses of just a few of these migrants' lives and to propose that we can use their stories as the basis for a broader understanding of the patterns and motivations for migration across the medieval Mediterranean. I do not argue that medieval migration and modern migration are exactly the same but, in accord with the goals of this Past Imperfect series to inspire new ways of thinking about the past, I want to draw attention to the migration experiences of medieval people.

In fact, one of the notable conclusions that I hope you will draw from reading the short biographies of these medieval migrants is the similarity of their motivations to those of today's migrants. The decision to leave one's home and travel into the unknown is not easily taken, neither today nor in the past, and typically only results from dire circumstances. Regime change, religious or political oppression, and the hope of finding a more successful and profitable life rank at the top of these motivations for medieval people. Others moved against their will—as enslaved individuals or as communities relocated or expelled by kings. Not discussed in this book are the many medieval travellers who relocated temporarily for reasons of business, diplomacy, or pilgrimage—this book is not about travel broadly, but about people who sought new lives in new lands as do today's immigrants and refugees. One key take-away that I hope you will get from these stories is the common humanity shared by medieval people and modern people. We may not know as much about their lives, but medieval migrants were *humans* who sought better circumstances for themselves and their families—just as modern migrants do.

A few caveats must be kept in mind as we progress through these migrants' mini-biographies. Most obviously, the majority of stories that I have been able to locate are representative of elite migrants and those whose journeys ended in successful adaptation to new circumstances. Very seldom do we find information about poor or otherwise disadvantaged people who sought refuge in new places, or those who died in the midst of their migration. This might be because migration opportunities typically only presented themselves to those with the means to pay for them and to set up a new life in a foreign place. Or, it might be the result of our primary source texts which, as a general rule for the medieval period, favour the social elite. In many cases (although not all of them), I think that we can safely extrapolate from an individual elite migrant to the broader circumstances that may have similarly motivated masses of lower-status refugees, although whether they would have been able to pay for travel and the establishment of new homes is a different and much more difficult question.

A second difficulty that will soon become obvious is that the majority of the migrants profiled here are men. This factor surely arises both from the biases of our sources and also from the fact that medieval women rarely would have migrated alone, without the protection and assistance of their families. But the reverse is also true: most men did not migrate alone, but were accompanied by mothers, wives, sisters, and daughters. In many of our migrants' stories, the focus is on the famous man but we also can glimpse the family members who moved with him. We must work a little harder, then, to witness the experiences of women migrants and refugees—to find their burial sites, archaeological remains, and the hints of their stories that lay beneath those of the men who often take centre stage. We may never be able to recover all of the unique ways in which migration affected women and children, but we must always remember that they existed.

This book argues two main points: one, that by viewing the medieval period through the lens of long-distance migration, we can better understand the commonalities connecting medieval and modern people. And in doing so, we can see greater commonality between the two periods than we might expect. Both medieval and modern eras have seen refugees seeking safer and better lives in new places, often for strikingly similar reasons. It is my hope that this work will help us to think anew about the long history of human migration, drawing closer together our perspectives on modern migrants and medieval ones. While the political conditions of the contemporary world and those of the Middle Ages are radically different—with distinct perspectives on the nature of borders, nationhood, place, and identity—nonetheless, we see human struggles and motivations for migration that share some common themes across the centuries.

A second perspective that this book seeks to advance is that patterns of migration, and the stories of individual migrants, can be an entry point for thinking about medieval Mediterranean history as a whole. Mediterranean studies has been a vibrant and growing field in recent decades, in large part because of the appeal of studying a place with no fixed boundaries, national identity, common language or religion, nor a monolithic culture or economy. But despite this attention, debate continues over what exactly the medieval Mediterranean *was*—one place or many, united by frequent and easy overseas communication or divided by religion and culture? One of the foundational historians of the Mediterranean, Fernand Braudel, writing in the mid-twentieth century, argued for a long continuity of stable structures across expanses of space and time. On the other hand, the early twentieth-century medievalist Henri Pirenne emphasized discontinuity: he argued for a decisive break between a unified Roman Mediterranean and a fractured one of the early medieval period; he located that division along a Muslim–Christian religio-cultural border. Both Braudel's and Pirenne's theories have been intensively debated ever since.

Early in the twenty-first century, three big books offered new approaches to the earlier paradigms. A challenge to Braudel came in *The Corrupting Sea* by Peregrine Horden and Nicholas Purcell. They argued that, rather than continuity based on shared geography and environment, it was in fact regional diversity (among what they call "micro-ecologies") that fuelled connections across the sea. People mitigated risk of food insecurity and managed their material needs through exchanges with people living in different environments. Because sailing around the Mediterranean was relatively easy and smooth, they argued, it was an ideal arena for frequent, small-scale connections. Michael McCormick's *Origins of the European Economy*, on the other hand, sought to answer Pirenne: it presented evidence of much greater travel and exchange than Pirenne allowed—especially between Christian and Islamic domains—using discrete anecdotes about cross-Mediterranean movements of people or items. Individual acts of travel or exchange, considered independently, may prove little, but in the aggregate they can show underlying patterns of movement, connection, and commerce. Stepping back from such systemic or structural approaches, David Abulafia, in his *The Great Sea*, emphasized the human plane of the Mediterranean Sea. He frames the phases of Mediterranean history in terms of how people used the sea—when and to what degree their exchanges, conflicts, and conversations united it and made it one coherent unit. Beyond the structural, environmental, or geographic elements, he asserted, it was individual and collective agency that shaped the human experience of the sea over centuries and even millennia.

Similarly, this book presents a Mediterranean on which individual people lived, worked, and sought security for their families. Their decisions, their motivations, and their experiences can form the basis for understanding the broader sweep of medieval Mediterranean history—one in which enduring structures and key events are played out in both large-scale population movements and the ground-level experiences of individuals and their families. But in a short book like this, certain choices had to be made; therefore, not every century, theme, path of migration, or important upheaval is featured here. Nonetheless, starting in the seventh and ending in the thirteenth century, many of the important developments in Mediterranean history are represented in these profiles. The events that inspired these migrations are some of the key moments in Mediterranean history: conquests, mass conversions, climactic changes, and economic revolutions. By studying cross-Mediterranean migration in the medieval period, and by focusing on the lived experiences of migrants, I think we can understand the history of that time and place in new ways.

This book is also written for people who have asked historical questions about cross-Mediterranean migration: is this only a modern phenomenon or is there a historical element to it? How did pre-modern people think about issues of homeland and the loss of identity when trying to establish a new life elsewhere? Perhaps one might also ask whether walls or boundaries worked in the Middle Ages to slow or halt migration, or whether medieval history might inform our modern understanding of border walls. This book cannot definitively answer that last question, since it concerns a period in which the notion of state borders was very different than ours. However, we will see herein numerous examples of people who moved across barriers that might seem as impenetrable as walls or modern state borders—those of religion, language, or political allegiance, for example. And while they did not have to confront passport control kiosks, hostile coast guards, or immigration officers, we will see that for many medieval migrants the process of establishing a new life in a new land was fraught with difficulties, dangers, and obstructions similar in many ways to those of modern refugees. Others, however, appear to have found successful lives and profitable positions in new places.

Proceeding in roughly chronological order, we first look at Christian refugees fleeing the Muslim conquest of the Levant, some of whom rose to prominence within the Roman Church in Italy. We then move to two Christian clerics, Theodore and Hadrian, from the Near East and North Africa respectively, both of whom migrated to early medieval England in order to take up senior positions in the Christian church based at Canterbury. While these men were appointed to England by the pope in Rome, archaeological evidence from the same centuries shows that they were by no means the only individuals from the Mediterranean Sea region who moved northward to live and work in the British Isles. In fact, early medieval England appears to have been closely linked to the Mediterranean region through economy, culture, travel, and migration.

From England, we move to Sicily, an island this book will return to several times. Situated at a vital geographical crossing point between the eastern and western basins of the Mediterranean Sea, and between its northern and southern shores, Sicily was regularly conquered, settled, and resettled throughout the Middle Ages. Ruled in turn by Roman emperors, Byzantine governors, Muslim emirs, and Latin kings, Sicily also housed a shifting and mixed population of Jews, Christians (Greek and Latin), and both Arab and Amazigh Muslims across this period. In these ways, it can show us some broad patterns of demographic change. Sicily also featured a number of active ports which were connected to sealanes going in all directions across the Mediterranean, meaning that travellers and migrants often found themselves passing through the island simply because many ships did so.

Just as we have seen in recent years the distressing images of refugees trying to reach the shores of Lampedusa or Sicily in ramshackle boats, so our case-studies show that Sicily has been a prominent destination for migration for a long time.[3] But medieval migration patterns were remarkably multi-directional: they did not necessarily flow northward

---

3 For an archaeological study of the modern Tunisia to Sicily crossing and its long history, see Emma Blake and Robert Schon, "The Archaeology of Contemporary Migrant Journeys in Western Sicily," *Journal of Mediterranean Archaeology* 32, no. 2 (2019): 173–94. Thanks to Sharon Kinoshita for bringing this article to my attention.

from Africa to Europe, as we might perceive modern ones to do. In fact, they often flowed in many directions at once, and Sicily was often a crossroads for both individual migrations and larger demographic shifts. First, we look at a young man who would come to be known as St. Elias the Younger, a Greek Christian Sicilian captured and enslaved by Muslim raiders. His initial migration away from the island was involuntary, but after escaping from the Christian family in North Africa who purchased him, he travelled widely throughout the Mediterranean and eventually returned to Sicily—by then a fully Muslim-controlled island.

The next chapter treats a man who voluntarily migrated in the opposite direction: Constantine the African moved from North Africa to Norman-held southern Italy. He greatly enriched the intellectual culture there by bringing Arabic medical books and knowledge, then translating them into Latin—making him a key figure in the development of early medieval medical and scientific knowledge in Europe. Constantine's story highlights the intellectual contributions that can be made by immigrants, and the transformative impact many medieval migrants had on their new home societies.

Next I return to Sicily, with several biographies of emigrants from the island during the turbulent years of the Norman conquest and their early kingdom. As Latin Christian invaders took over progressively more of the island's Muslim-ruled territory, the demographics of the entire Mediterranean region shifted dramatically. Jewish merchants, the subject of the first of these chapters, were active traders between Sicily and the northern shores of Africa; many of them chose to flee the island in search of safer homes. Their stories show that migration was often multi-directional, even while it was nearly always filled with uncertainty. A unique discovery of documents and letters sent among this mercantile community, called the Cairo Geniza, allows us to witness their fears and the dangers of migration up close. This chapter is followed by one about merchants as a group, both Jewish and Christian, who often relied upon their knowledge of foreign places and cultures to establish new lives abroad.

In contrast to the Jews whose stories are told in their own words, the Muslims who emigrated away from newly Christian Sicily are typically only seen in retrospect. We know, for example, of Muslim scholars and poets whose families traced their origins to Sicily, and who may have departed the island because of the Norman conquest but their biographies do not explicitly tell us so. One example is the Muslim jurist Imam al-Mazari, who lived and worked in North Africa but who issued judgments related to the Muslim community still living in Sicily. He, like other scholars and poets, such as Ibn Hamdis, maintained an identity that was closely connected with Sicily, long after their emigration. The final chapter on people immigrating away from Norman Sicily concerns the Muslims who did not get the chance to depart, despite their desire to do so. Focusing on one young woman who sought marriage with a foreign visitor in order to escape the island, this chapter also examines the migration experiences of women in general. It was always difficult for women to migrate alone, and it is also more difficult to access women's stories of migration and its effects.

Even while Jews and Muslims were departing from Sicily, the Norman conquerors encouraged Christian immigration to the island. The final chapter about Sicily is centred on the story of George of Antioch, a Greek Christian who found his way to the Norman Kingdom of Sicily and ascended to high rank there. But he was not the only Christian who moved to Sicily at the time: this chapter also presents Latin immigrants from northern Europe. In this period, it is clear that immigration was being managed by the Normans as a way of altering their island's demographics in ways that served their purposes.

Just like the Jews who left an increasingly hostile Sicily, the Jewish intellectual Moses Maimonides emigrated from Iberia after its conquest by the Alhomads from North Africa. The story of Maimonides demonstrates both the difficulty of finding a safe place to migrate to and also the emotional impact of migration. But, unlike the Jews who were forced out of increasingly homogenizing Christian monarchies of western Europe over the twelfth-fifteenth centuries, Maimonides and his family immigrated out of a desire to live and worship among co-religionists rather than among a hostile majority culture.

The final profile returns to those who desired to live among people who shared their religious faith, this time as religious converts. Although most changes in religion came about as part of the demographic shifts that followed conquests and regime changes, some medieval individuals made the radical choice to adopt a non-dominant religion. When they did so, they usually also chose to relocate, both in order to avoid persecution from the community into which they were born and also in order to live and learn from co-religionists.

While these few stories by no means cover all of the migrants from the Middle Ages, I consider them representative of the primary motives for migration in the period. And while reading them, I hope you will keep in mind what they have to teach us about both the Middle Ages and today. Specifically, their stories help challenge some commonly-held assumptions about immigrants and migration. First, I have in mind the assumption that migration pathways always bring people towards Europe. In fact, these biographies show multi-directional movements crisscrossing the Mediterranean, with groups sometimes moving nearly simultaneously in opposite directions. Second, these stories challenge the assumption that refugees have nothing to offer the society to which they immigrate. To the contrary, we find numerous cases in which immigrants brought with them intellectual and artisanal expertise, valued goods and products, and much-needed skills and experience. And third, they contradict the assumption that migration disrupts an otherwise racially pure status quo, even though some foreign immigrants may have faced racialized hatred and hostility.

Just as it is today, migration in the Middle Ages was filled with danger, uncertainty, and difficulties of assimilation. But as you read these profiles, I hope you will see the ways that medieval migrants and modern ones alike represent a common yearning for safety and a profitable and secure livelihood—even if that meant uprooting a life and moving across land and sea to find a new home.

Chapter 1

Refugees from the Islamic Conquests

SEVENTH-CENTURY LEVANT

Many migration stories begin with war, destruction, and violence. In many cases throughout history, the violent effects of conquest and regime change have led to massive demographic upheavals and the death, enslavement, or forced relocation of many people. Raids, conquests, and wars also impact surviving populations who remain in place, often destroying their cities and homes, undermining their ways of life, and hindering their continued economic subsistence. To be sure, not every conquest throughout history has resulted in waves of out-migration—at least as far as our sources can demonstrate. And it is demonstrably true that many surviving people whose lands were conquered found ways to live peaceably under new authorities, either as religious and linguistic minorities or as cultural or religious converts. But a majority of the migration stories in this book start with regime change, conquest, or episodes of unendurable violence—even though many of the surviving texts do not themselves record the acts of violence that inspired the migration events themselves.

One of the most historically important conquests of the early Middle Ages was the Islamic takeover of the eastern and southern shores of the Mediterranean Sea, much of which took place during the seventh century. Muslim troops moved out of the Arabian peninsula and, within a decade of the Prophet Muhammad's death (in 632 CE), had captured important Christian-ruled cities such as Damascus and Jerusalem, along with their surrounding countryside. And while those cities had been conquered and re-conquered by the Byzantine Greek and Persian Sassanid Empires over preceding decades, the Muslim takeover is the one that would last throughout the Middle Ages. Those Arab-Muslim forces then moved in multiple directions, wresting all of northern Africa from Roman (Byzantine) control and all of Iraq and Iran from Persian domain.

Some seventh-century texts in Greek, Syriac, and Coptic record Christian reactions to the violence and population dislocations of the Islamic conquests. Patriarch Sophronius, for example, the leader of the Christian Church in Jerusalem, preached a Christmas sermon circa 634 during which he bemoaned the fear and destruction that Muslim raids were having on the people of the region.[1] He claimed that the warfare made pilgrims unable to reach the city's holy sites and described the terror and grief that characterized their anticipation of further attacks. They were, he said, "bound by fear of the Saracens. We are like Adam banned from paradise, though we do not see the twisting flaming sword, but rather the wild and barbarous Saracen [sword], which is filled with every diabolical savagery" (Hoyland, 70). Fear of conquest violence seems to have been a significant issue among Jerusalem's Christian population, even if the sermon used elevated rhetoric and racialized slurs to evoke a strong response among its listeners.

A few years later, in another sermon, Sophronius pondered: "Why do barbarian raids abound? Why are the troops of the Saracens attacking us? Why has there been so much destruction and plunder? Why are there incessant outpourings of human blood? Why are the birds of the sky devouring human bodies? Why have churches been pulled down?" (Hoyland, 72). And the Muslims, he continues, "overrun the places which are not allowed to them, plunder cities, devastate

---

1 Robert Hoyland, *Seeing Islam as Others Saw It: A Survey and Evaluation of Christian, Jewish and Zoroastrian Writings on Early Islam* (Princeton: Darwin, 1997), 67–73.

fields, burn down villages, set on fire the holy churches, over-
turn the sacred monasteries, oppose the Byzantine armies
arrayed against them, and in fighting raise up the trophies [of
war] and add victory to victory" (Hoyland, 72–73). Again, we
can look underneath the dramatic phrasing to some kind of
reality of violence and fear of violence. Only a year or so later,
in 637, Sophronius's worst fears came true, as he presided
over the surrender of the holy city of Jerusalem, its churches,
and many of its holy relics to 'Umar (634–44), the second
caliph and leader of the invading Muslim armies.

Other early witnesses to the Muslim armies' progress
describe similar feelings of fear, confusion, and panic in
the face of destructive attacks. One account claims that in
a single year four thousand poor villagers were killed, not
only Christians but also Jews and Samaritans, "and the Arabs
destroyed the whole region."[2] Similarly, John of Nikiu, a Coptic
bishop who described the destructions of the Muslim invasion
of Egypt, claimed that when they conquered a town "they
compelled the city to open its gates, and they put to the
sword all that surrendered, and they spared none, whether
old men, babe, or woman."[3] And, because many of the surviving texts were written by Christian ecclesiastical figures,
many of these early sources describe the massacres of monasteries full of monks and nuns, in addition to towns, fields,
and churches.

Monks and other religious people were certainly not the
only victims of violence and dislocation in the wake of the
Muslim raids in Syria–Palestine or across northern Africa, but
they may have been the ones best positioned to migrate to
safety. Because they had both education and established

2 "Chronicle ad 640," trans. Michael Philip Penn, in Penn, *When Christians First Met Muslims: A Sourcebook of the Earliest Syriac Writings on Islam* (Berkeley: University of California Press, 2015), 25–28.

3 *The Chronicle of John (c. 690 A.D.), Coptic Bishop of Nikiu*, ed. and transl. Robert Henry Charles (London: Williams & Norgate, 1916; repr. Amsterdam: APA/Philo, 1981), 179 (c. CXI–CXX.34).

ecclesiastical posts, many churchmen from conquered lands were able to find places in monasteries or within the church hierarchy in another city. They often maintained personal connections with people overseas because they travelled to other cities—such as Antioch, Constantinople, and Rome—for education or on pilgrimage to holy sites, giving them knowledge of travel and foreign lands, as well as contacts that they could rely upon to help them get established in a new land after their migration.

In fact, several seventh- and eighth-century migrants from the eastern Mediterranean region ended their careers at the very top of the Latin Church's hierarchy: as popes in Rome. These men and their families engaged in the kind of multi-stage migration that we will see in many later migrants' stories, suggesting that this was a common pattern for medieval refugees seeking new places to live: that is, it was not always the first place they disembarked that ended up being home. Popes such as Conon (686–87) and Sergius I (687–701) migrated from the eastern Mediterranean first to Sicily and thence to Rome. Sicily, as we will see several times throughout this book, has long been a landing spot for refugees seeking to migrate across the Mediterranean—whether the direction of that flight was northward, southward, eastward, or westward.

Dated as they are to the mid-to-late seventh century, these men and their families must have migrated because of the Muslim conquests described by authors like Sophronius of Jerusalem and John of Nikiu. Conon was a Greek who had been born in Asia Minor but educated in Sicily, so we must presume that he was a youth when his family who chose to migrate, although we do not know exactly why or when.[4] Sergius likewise was raised and educated in Sicily, but we know that his father Tiberius was from Syria and had migrated from Antioch. The timing suggests that he and his family departed

---

4 *Life* of Pope Conon (686–87), in *Liber Pontificalis: texte, introduction et commentaire* [hereafter *LP*], ed. L. Duchesne and C. Vogel, 3 vols. (Paris: de Boccard, 1955–57), I.LXXXV, c. 157.

at the time of the Muslim takeover of that region: Antioch came under Muslim control in 638.[5] During these centuries, migration from eastern Christian territories, training in the Greek Church, and education in the Greek language were clearly not barriers to ascending the hierarchy of the Roman Latin Church. Their status as migrants obviously did not hinder their advancement in Rome.

Sicily at the time of these popes was a Greek-held island, with close political and cultural ties to its imperial capital at Constantinople, but with a sizeable population of Latin Christians. Sicily was also home to extensive lands owned directly by the popes, meaning that they were closely involved in the administration and economy of the island. Numerous churches and monasteries using the Latin liturgy made it possible for Greek Christians to learn the practices and texts required to participate in Roman services. Such an arrangement provided Greek churchmen with opportunities to become familiar with the Latin ecclesiastical world, which seems to have given several immigrant men the opportunity to rise to this highest post in the Roman Church. Sicily thus acted as a helpful way-station on the longer paths of migration for men whose families were fleeing the Muslim invasions of eastern Mediterranean lands.

The scanty nature of our sources for these immigrant popes' lives means that we often have no more than a sentence or even just a few words about their origins; their families are almost entirely absent from the record. If we read between the lines, however, we can glimpse the women and children who must have been part of these refugee families. For Greek-speaking popes raised in Sicily, their mothers may well have migrated as well as their fathers, along with unnamed siblings and likely much larger family groups. Tiberius is the only family member named among these biographies, showing clearly how much family background has been left out by their papal biographers. Mothers, sisters, and other family members who may have also been part of these

---

5 *Life* of Pope Sergius I (687–701), *LP* I.LXXXVI, c. 158, l.1–2.

migrations can only be imagined. Similarly, we can only guess at how they must have felt as their homes and churches were destroyed by invading armies, prompting them to seek safety across the sea.

Sicily was a regular recipient of migrants in the early medieval period, just as it is today. It had established shipping connections with ports in the eastern and southern Mediterranean, making it an easy place to which to find passage on a ship. And just like today, it served as a kind of bridge between Europe, northern Africa, and the eastern Mediterranean. It was also politically important as a node of connection between the two main centres of Christian life, Constantinople and Rome. The stories of popes like Conon and Sergius—although we know few details about their lives or migration experiences—show how this often worked in practice.

Chapter 2

Hadrian and Theodore

SEVENTH-CENTURY ENGLAND

Two other seventh-century men undertook migrations similar to those of the Syrian and Greek popes, fleeing the Muslim conquests in the Levant and moving westward. But these two men went even further than Rome, eventually moving all the way to England, where they became two of the most important Christian leaders in early medieval England. Their routes of migration, through Italy, highlights the central role that the Roman Christian Church played in the lives of those seeking advancement in ecclesiastical careers. It also shows the indirect and multi-stage nature of many paths of migration. Their reasons for movement—a mix of regime change, flight from danger, and travel for education and career advancement— also echo the migration stories of many other migrants whose stories remain available to historians.

Theodore of Tarsus, as he was known in early English sources, was appointed archbishop of Canterbury—the highest ecclesiastical office in that land—by Pope Vitalian (657-72). Originally, as his name suggests, he was from the region of greater Syria, which was under Byzantine control until a series of conquests in the early seventh century. Born in the city of Tarsus in 602 and probably educated in Antioch, Theodore came from a Greek Christian family. Conquests by the Persian Sassanid Empire (613-14) and then, about two decades later, by the expanding Muslim state removed the Levantine coast from the Greek cultural and political orbit. At the time of the Persian conquest, Theodore would have been around twelve years old, and well into adulthood when the Muslim conquerors took Tarsus in 637. Extant sources do not tell us exactly when he and his family left the area, but the chronology of his life and education suggests that they may have migrated away from Syria around the time of the Muslim conquest.

For someone like Theodore, educated in the Greek tradition and seeking a career in the Church, life under Muslim control and the destruction to the region's ecclesiastical structures may have seemed unbearable. Many monks from the Syria–Palestine area fled after these conquests, many to Sicily and southern Italy or to Rome or Constantinople. It should be noted, however, that not all highly-educated Christian thinkers and administrators made such a choice. Prominent early Christian figures like John of Damascus (676–749), a younger contemporary of Theodore and Hadrian, belonged to a family that chose to remain in their homes and administrative positions after the change of regime. John may have followed his father in serving the new Muslim administration in Damascus, although we know very little about John's career as a civil servant. More well known is that he ended his life as a monk in the monastery of Mar Saba, near Jerusalem, writing prolifically on Christian theology. John, his family, and his fellow monks attest to the continued presence of Christian communities and ecclesiastical structures in the newly Muslim region.

But Theodore represents those who elected to move away from the Muslim-controlled Levant, migrating first to Constantinople and thence to Rome (in the 660s). These two cities were the most significant centres of learning and ecclesiastical advancement in the Christian world, and Theodore's movement between them mirrors that of many other learned Christians of both Latin and Greek traditions. What we do not know is specifically why Theodore left Constantinople to move to Rome, rather than establishing his career within the hierarchy of the Greek Church. His theological positions later came to align with those of the Roman Church, so perhaps he migrated to Rome because of theological disputes with other Greek Christians.

In Rome, Theodore seems to have joined a community of Greek monks and began learning Latin literature. Thus deeply educated in both Greek and Latin traditions (and possibly also a native speaker of the Syriac language), he came to the attention of the Roman hierarchy. There is strong evidence to suggest that Theodore was engaged in doctrinal debates (about the Byzantine doctrine of monotheletism) and participated in a Lateran Council in 649, which was called by Pope Martin I (649–55) to compose a formal statement condemning and opposing the doctrine. This debate was deadly, resulting in the arrest, trial, and exile of Pope Martin by Byzantine officials. Political exile was a regular practice among the Byzantines, who often sent their enemies to Mediterranean islands that were far from the capital or from their seats of power. Martin was exiled from Italy first to Constantinople and then to Cherson in the Crimea.

Theodore, broadly educated and deeply involved in current religio-political affairs, became a significant figure in the seventh-century Roman Church. So when a new leader of the Church in England was needed in 668, Pope Vitalian appointed Theodore as archbishop of Canterbury. He travelled from Rome with another migrant from across the Mediterranean named Hadrian. It is reported that Hadrian was the pope's first choice, but he turned down the archiepiscopal position and suggested Theodore instead. The two men arrived in Canterbury in May 669 and embarked on a project of systematizing English liturgical and practical matters, bringing English Christianity into closer alignment with Rome. They also created a school in Canterbury where students were taught not only matters of Christian doctrine and practice, but also poetry, astronomy, and other subjects. These were topics regularly studied and taught in the schools of Greek and Islamicate regions, so Theodore and Hadrian had educational advantages that were welcomed and appreciated in England.

Hadrian, Theodore's companion in travel and in service to the English church, had likewise been an immigrant to Italy from across the Mediterranean Sea. Bede, in his *Ecclesiasti-*

cal History (ca. 825) called him "a man of the African nation" ("vir natione Afir"), which some historians have interpreted as meaning that he was of Amazigh (often called Berber) descent, an Indigenous community from the area of modern Libya.[1] Perhaps he too had fled in the wake of invading Muslim armies, which moved across North Africa in the seventh century and conquered all of the Maghrib (northern Africa to the west of Egypt) between 647 and 709, but we do not know for sure.

Hadrian and Theodore are like so many other migrants who established successful lives in Latin Europe—they retained the monikers that allow us to glimpse their place of origin, but very little else of their backstories remains to us. For so many of these migrants, the medieval texts through which we learn about them do not record much information about their migration stories or about life before their big move. What we do know is that Hadrian found his way to southern Italy, much like Theodore, and there rose to high ecclesiastical office. Thus, he too must have had a significant Christian education and a career in the church as well as connections to help establish his new life in Italy.

In Italy, Hadrian eventually became an abbot at Naples before Pope Vitalian asked him to accompany Theodore to England, where the two would craft a program of reform that helped shape the Christian church in England. Bede tells us that Hadrian was initially reluctant to leave Italy and relocate to England. We are not given details about the nature of that reluctance, but he eventually agreed to go, and so the two men travelled together from Rome to England, where Hadrian became the abbot of St. Peter's and St. Paul's at Canterbury. He lived and worked in England for four decades before dying in 709. Theodore had died in 690 after twenty-two years as archbishop. Together, Hadrian and Theodore introduced early medieval England to new concepts in science, exegesis,

---

1 Bede, *Bede's Ecclesiastical History of the English People*, ed. and trans. Bertram Colgrave and R. A. B. Mynors (Oxford: Clarendon Press, 1969), bk. 4, chap. 1.

medicine, and other intellectual pursuits. They were the only known Greek-speakers on the island, but it is unclear how much Greek language or literature they taught to their students. Administratively and intellectually, however, it is quite clear that these two migrants from across the Mediterranean helped to bring early medieval England closer to Rome and to the intellectual world of the Greek East.

These two men, however, were by no means the only ones active in connecting the early medieval Mediterranean to the British Isles. Pottery evidence from archaeological sites demonstrates that, between the fifth and seventh centuries, trade goods from the eastern Mediterranean were being imported to the western and southwestern regions of England and Wales, and that some of the people responsible for conducting that trade may have stayed and settled there.[2] Byzantine pottery finds in England suggest that a wide variety of Mediterranean food products were being exchanged for locally-made metalwork and glass beads. Isotope analysis of elements found in the teeth of humans buried in early medieval cemeteries on the Welsh coast demonstrates that a significant number of them were immigrants—some from other parts of the British Isles, and others from much farther away. While it is difficult for current science to isolate the exact origins of these migrants who lived and died in southern Wales, in combination with historical and archaeological evidence it has been suggested that some were from western Ireland and a few were from sunnier and warmer climates, such as the Mediterranean region from which the pottery and food items were imported. Because these individuals were buried at several different cemeteries in Wales, and because they included women and children, it may be surmised that these Mediterranean immigrants were not isolated examples but were, in fact, part of larger population movements from the Mediterranean northward to the British Isles. And while

---

2 K. A. Hemer et al., "Evidence of Early Medieval Trade and Migration between Wales and the Mediterranean Sea Region," *Journal of Archaeological Science* 40 (2013): 2352–59.

some of those migrants may have been the traders responsible for bringing valued import goods from the Mediterranean, others may have included both family units and women who migrated and then intermarried with the local population.

Similar results have come from tests on skeletal remains at archaeological sites in the northeast of England. At least half of the individuals in one early medieval burial site in Northumbria, near the famous monastery of Lindisfarne, were of nonlocal origin.[3] Burial goods from some of the graves suggest a birthplace in Scandinavia, consistent with historical evidence for waves of migration and raiding on English shores by Norse and Germanic peoples. But isotopic analysis shows that a good many of the individuals buried there were from other parts of the British Isles, Ireland, or continental Europe. One group of burials, comprised of one man, three women, and three children, show strong evidence of having been born in the Mediterranean region. Archaeologists believe that they could have been "economic migrants"—perhaps traders like those who came to Wales with Byzantine goods, or artisans who were brought in to help build castles and monasteries in the region and who moved their families with them. Whatever brought these different families to the British Isles, studies like these demonstrate that Hadrian and Theodore were far from being the only immigrants to the British Isles from the Mediterranean region during the early medieval period.

As scientific methods of studying medieval populations improve, it is likely that more evidence for histories of migration will be found. Currently, researchers using ancient DNA (aDNA), for example, are investigating the origins of individual people buried in gravesites in sixth-century northern Italy and Hungary.[4] Similar work on modern genetic material can

---

3 S. E. Groves, et al., "Mobility Histories of 7th–9th Century AD People Buried at Early Medieval Bamburgh, Northumberland, England," *American Journal of Physical Anthropology* 151 (2013): 462–76.

4 See https://genetichistory.ias.edu for an overview and C. E. G. Amorim et al., "Understanding 6th-century Barbarian Social

help to illuminate some of the migration history of broad populations. For instance, broad DNA studies of modern Sicilians reveal strong historical connections to populations of Greeks, Tunisian Amazigh, other North African populations, the Norse (Normans), and Arabs.[5] These types of scientific methods can profitably be combined with archaeological work and study of the written record to demonstrate the paths and patterns of population movements in the premodern world. They cannot, however, resuscitate the lived experiences that prompted and attended the migration events themselves.

Organization and Migration through Paleogenomics," *Nature Communications* 9, art. no. 3547 (2018): unpag., https://doi.org/10.1038/s41467-018-06024-4.

5 Cornelia Di Gaetano et al., "Differential Greek and Northern African Migrations to Sicily are Supported by Genetic Evidence from the Y Chromosome," *European Journal of Human Genetics* 17 (2009): 91–99; Cristian Capelli et al., "Moors and Saracens in Europe: Estimating the Medieval North African Male Legacy in Southern Europe," *European Journal of Human Genetics* 17 (2009): 848–52.

Chapter 3

St. Elias the Younger

NINTH-CENTURY SICILY AND NORTH AFRICA

Many broad trends in cross-Mediterranean migration are best illustrated by examining the island of Sicily, which sent and received immigrants in all directions across the medieval period. Many of these developments were related to the repeated political and military conquests of the island. From the early sixth century, Sicily was a Greek-controlled island under the dominion of Constantinople, but by the late seventh century, it was experiencing semi-regular attacks along its southern shores launched from Muslim-ruled North Africa. For the first century and a half of these raids, it appears that the attackers were seeking booty and slaves and then returning to North Africa. But after several decades of seaborne attacks, interspersed with periods of diplomatic peace, they turned their attentions to conquest and settlement of the island. And alongside political conquest came significant changes in demographics, some through conquest and settlement, others through emigration and flight from danger.

From the very earliest years of Muslim rule in North Africa, military forays also went out into the Mediterranean Sea. Using the naval fleets that they took over in the conquered Byzantine ports of both Egypt and Ifriqiya (Arabic for "North Africa," a region roughly equivalent to modern Tunisia and parts of Libya and Algeria), Muslim forces raided the Mediterranean islands of Sicily, Sardinia, Crete, and nearby smaller islands. From possibly as early as the 650s (the dates are disputed), Muslim forces began attacking the southern shores of

Sicily. Most of these raids were just that—quick strikes meant to obtain booty and slaves and then return to their home base. We find no evidence in the sources that these earliest assaults were intended to conquer or rule Sicilian territory, although the suspicion is that if they had found it possible to do so they would, indeed, have captured the island. As it was, these raids continued throughout the seventh and eighth centuries and only transformed into an attempt at outright military takeover in 827.

Over the course of the seventh and eighth centuries, Greek Sicily was connected to Constantinople through networks of administration and culture, to European power-centres through military and political communications, to Rome via Church structures, and, at the same time, to Muslim North Africa through these patterns of military raid. At the same time, however, the connections between Byzantine Sicily and Aghlabid Ifriqiya were not only violent in nature: diplomatic and economic connections also flourished between the two regions. In other words, ships sailed in both directions across the Strait of Sicily for a wide variety of reasons and carrying cargoes and passengers of many types.

In terms of the military raids, texts in both Greek and Arabic describe ships full of soldiers arriving on Sicily's shores, raiding towns and monasteries, and returning to North Africa with enslaved people and bejewelled icons and other ecclesiastical treasures. Greek saints' biographies describe the population fleeing in terror to fortified places, caves, hilltop towns, and monastic settlements either further north in Sicily or on the Italian mainland. One Latin source, the biography of Pope Adeodatus II, describes a raid in 669 that was thought to have originated in Alexandria and was directed at the city of Syracuse, the Byzantine provincial capital.[1] The population of Syracuse fled to fortresses and into the mountains for safety, but many were slaughtered. The Muslims took plunder in the form of bronze (possibly ecclesiastical objects) and then returned to Alexandria. Similar stories continue to be

---

[1] *Life* of Pope Adeodatus II (672–76): *LP* I.LXXVIII, c. 137.

recorded throughout the eighth century, though most of the raids originated from Ifriqiya rather than Egypt.

Many Sicilians returned to their homes after the attackers departed, but others founded new settlements, homes, and monasteries further north in mainland Italy. Just like Christian refugees and migrants from the eastern Mediterranean, most of the people fleeing Sicily for whom we have records were saints and churchmen, due to the disproportionate survival of ecclesiastical texts. Examples of permanent migration are found in several of the Greek saints' lives written in Italy. St. Leo-Luke of Corleone (ca. 815–915), for example, was born in the Sicilian town of Corleone (an inland town a short distance south of Palermo) sometime in the early ninth century.[2] As a young man, he entered the monastery of St. Philip of Agira, on the western edge of Mount Etna. But when that monastery and its region became targets for the Muslim raids, Leo-Luke and many of his fellow monks moved northward to Calabria, the "toe" of Italy.

Another Greek saint, known as Joseph the Hymnographer (d. ca. 886) also fled from Sicily because of Muslim raids, but he moved eastward—first to the Peloponnesos and thence to Constantinople.[3] There, he established himself in a career in the church and was sent to Rome as an emissary, although he never made it to his destination. Onboard the ship toward Rome, Joseph encountered hostile Muslim naval forces and was taken captive; his biographer claims that his captors were Muslim pirates. He was held hostage on Crete, an island

---

2 *Vita Leonis Lucae Corilionensis Abbatis, BHL* [*Bibliotheca hagiographica latina antiquae et mediae aetatis*] 4842; *AASS* [*Acta Sanctorum*] March I, 98–102. Latin edition and Italian translation by Maria Stelladoro, *La Vita di San Leone Luca di Corleone* (Grottaferrata: Badia Greca di Grottaferrata, 1995).

3 Theophanes the Monk, *Vita Iosephi hymnographi, BHG* [*Bibliotheca hagiographica graeca*] 944–47b; *AASS* vol. 10, April III, 266–76, in *Monumenta graeca et latina ad historiam Photii patriarchae pertinentia*, ed. A. Papadopoulos-Kerameus, 2 vols. (St. Petersburg: Kirschbaum, 1899–1901), 2:1–14.

that had been under Muslim control from the 820s. Later he was ransomed and returned to Constantinople. Leo-Luke and Joseph represent the two major pathways taken by emigrants from Sicily during the early Middle Ages: northward to mainland Italy or eastward to Constantinople.

At the same time, however, migration involving Sicily was not uni-directional—the island received as well as sent migrants. This was also a period of continued Muslim incursions into North Africa, and some Christians from there sought asylum in Byzantine Sicily. In 697/98, for example, a Muslim general captured the North African port of Carthage and, according to Muslim chronicler Ibn 'Idhari, some of the Christian and Berber residents of the city took refuge in Sicily, while others moved to Spain.[4] This confluence of people leaving the island and others arriving on it at roughly the same time (and due in part to similar forces acting in different locations) was repeated at other points in Sicily's history, and shows how the island could serve as a transitional spot for many people relocating within the western Mediterranean area. It also highlights the central role played by Sicily in larger trends of movement and communication in the early medieval Mediterranean.

But not all of the migrants to and from early medieval Sicily moved under their own volition. One of the Greek sources describes the abduction and enslavement of one of Sicily's Greek Christians, a man who would later be known as St. Elias the Younger of Enna (823–903).[5] His family, Christian nobil-

---

4 Ibn 'Idhārī, *Kitāb al-bayān al-Mughrib*, in *Biblioteca arabo-sicula*, ed. Michele Amari (Leipzig: Brockhaus, 1857–87), 2nd ed. Umberto Rizzitano, 2 vols. (Palermo: Accademia Nazaionale di Scienze Lettere e Arti, 1988) [hereafter *BAS* Arabic], 353; *Biblioteca arabo-sicula, versione italiana*, ed. Michele Amari, 2 vols. (Turin: Loescher, 1880–89), 2nd ed. Umberto Rizzitano et al., 3 vols. (Palermo: Accademia Nazaionale di Scienze Lettere e Arti, 1997–98) [hereafter *BAS* Ital.], 2:456.

5 *Vita Eliae Iunioris*, *BHG* 580; *AASS* vol. 37, August XVII, 479–509. Greek edition and Italian translation by Giuseppe Rossi Taibbi, *Vita di sant'Elia il Giovane* (Palermo: Istituto Siciliano di Studi Bizantini e Neoellenici, 1962).

ity from Enna, a hilltop town in the southcentral part of the island, had initially fled to a castle called Santa Maria in Calabria, southern Italy, in order to escape the Muslim attacks. According to the text, the raiders were said to have come from Carthage (meaning Ifriqiya) and destroyed the town of Enna, despite its relatively safe position at the top of a peak.

Despite his family's flight in search of a safe location, the child Elias was caught up in the raids and was captured twice by Muslims from North Africa. His biographer describes "Saracens" rushing up and overpowering him as he walked along. Elias' first period in Muslim captivity ended when a Byzantine ship intercepted the one on which he was being transported to North Africa. He was returned home to Sicily, only to be nabbed again in a subsequent Muslim attack on the island. The second time, he was taken to Ifriqiya as a slave and sold to a Christian family there. He escaped from his owners and then travelled throughout the Mediterranean world—including on pilgrimage to Jerusalem—before returning to Sicily. From there he went on a pilgrimage to Rome and then sailed toward Constantinople, but died en route.

A tale like Elias's illuminates a number of important elements of early medieval Sicily's history, and why it was the site of so much multi-directional migration. Elias' family fled northward to escape the violence, but returned when they believed that the coast was clear. Temporary relocation is a type of migration that is rarely witnessed in medieval sources, as is enslavement, in both cases likely because the interests of surviving texts lay elsewhere. Elias himself was forcibly removed from his home twice, both times captured and enslaved. Most of the early medieval people who were forced into slavery and relocated against their will do not show up in our sources as named individuals, if they appear at all. Elias' story is remarkable for allowing us to glimpse the human experience behind medieval enslavement.

Elias's story also demonstrates the intense pace of both voluntary and involuntary travel around the early medieval Mediterranean region. Although his departures from the island took place under force, once he had escaped enslavement, he travelled for pilgrimage and education to Jerusalem, Constantinople, and other important sites of Christian culture in the eastern Mediterranean, as well as to Rome. And his return to his native island as an adult—the biography tells us that he came back to visit his mother, who must by then have been quite elderly—was a voluntary visit to an island that had changed significantly since his capture as a child. Indeed, Elias landed on an island that was by that time mostly under Muslim control, having sailed on ships alongside Muslim passengers (miraculously converting some of them to Christianity). But, as is clear from other sources, he also came back to an island that had a notable Greek Christian population remaining despite the change in rulership: his family had, apparently, continued to live on the island, as had many monasteries full of Greek Christian monks and many towns' worth of Greek people.

We know, in fact, that many Greeks remained in Muslim Sicily for centuries, choosing neither to migrate nor to convert to Islam and assimilate to the dominant culture. The evidence for this lack of migration is found in sources chronicling the mid-eleventh century Latin Christian (Norman) conquest of the island (on which more below). When those Latin conquerors came upon communities of Greek Christians, they expected to be hailed as liberators. They were shocked, then, to discover that the Greeks were perfectly happy living as linguistic and religious minorities under the island's Muslim administration and that they viewed the Latins as unwelcome invaders.[6] Many Christians must have remained in conquered places, some likely assimilating or converting to Islam over time (although this process is virtually invisible to historians). But it is notable that enough Greek Christians remained in

---

6 Geoffrey of Malaterra, *De rebus gestis Rogerii Calabriae et Siciliae comitis et Robertis Guiscardi ducis fratris eius*, ed. Ernesto Pontieri, *Rerum Italicarum Scriptores* series 2, vol. 5 pt. 1 (Bologna: Zanichelli, 1927), bk. 2, chap. 14 and bk. 2, chap. 29. Translation in Kenneth Baxter Wolf, *The Deeds of Count Roger of Calabria and Sicily and of His Brother Duke Robert Guiscard* (Ann Arbor: University of Michigan Press, 2005), 92 and 102–4.

Muslim Sicily and resisted assimilation for them to have maintained their distinctive linguistic and religious traditions even after two hundred years.

The story of Elias the Younger represents many of the ways in which individuals moved and populations changed in the medieval Mediterranean. His life encompassed forced migration under enslavement, voluntary travel for pilgrimage and learning, and family members who chose not to (or were not able to) migrate away from a conquered land. His story shows the great mobility of Mediterranean life: even though at first he did not emigrate voluntarily, he appears to have spent the rest of his life travelling widely rather than settling in one place. And his life shows us both the hazards and the opportunities of travel across the sea, while it also bears witness to the major transformations taking place in the central Mediterranean during the ninth century.

Chapter 4

Constantine the African

ELEVENTH-CENTURY NORTH AFRICA AND
SOUTHERN ITALY

Just as migrants like Theodore and Hadrian enriched the intellectual and religious cultures of early medieval England, and like Elias participated in both pilgrimages and educational travel, another émigré from across the Mediterranean was a key figure in the development of early medieval medical and scientific knowledge in Europe. Without the influence of Constantine, known as "the African," early medieval Christian medical science would have been far more impoverished than it was. He introduced texts, ideas, and scientific knowledge that were unavailable and unknown by the Latins, translating a long list of books from Arabic that became central to the scientific study of medicine in the early medieval Latinate world. Constantine produced at least twenty-four and perhaps as many as thirty-four translations, all from Arabic into Latin, thus greatly enhancing early medieval knowledge about the human body, its ailments, and how to treat them.[1]

Like many of our other migrants, much of Constantine's life is obscured by omissions or fabrications in the existing sources. For instance, we do not know Constantine's ethnic origin, although we are fairly positive that he was born in Ifriqiya. Was he a descendent of Greeks or Copts who remained in Muslim northern Africa, or from an Arab or Ama-

---

1 Many thanks to both Monica Green and Eliza Glaze, who shared their insights with me and allowed me to read pre-publication versions of their scholarship on Constatine.

zigh family? Was "Constantine" even his birth name, or one he adopted upon baptism into the Christian religion? All we know is that his African origin was important enough to be attached to his name and his biography, and that it was a significant aspect of his self-presentation. Several of the texts he produced include the authorial autobiography "Ego Constantinus africanus montis cassinensis monacus" (I, Constantine the African, monk of Monte Cassino). We also know that his native language was Arabic and that he was well-versed in medical knowledge before his arrival in Italy.

Likewise, sources differ about the religion of his birth family, although we know that he ended his life as a monk at the Latin Christian Abbey of Monte Cassino, in southern Italy. This may well be a story of religious conversion as well as cross-cultural migration. Or, perhaps, he may have been born into an Arabic-speaking Christian community in northern Africa. Two of the biographies we have for him suggest that he had been born a Muslim. The third key text omits any discussion about his religious identity, perhaps suggesting that he was a Christian before his migration. And although stories about his motivation for migration do appear in the Latin texts about him, we cannot be exactly sure why he left his birthplace and moved to Latin Christian Europe because the texts differ so widely. Many of the stories we have about him contain aspects of fantasy that are not trusted by scholars and fail to answer questions that we might pose.

But, unlike many other refugees and migrants, we have more than one existing biography of Constantine, attesting to the importance that he held for early medieval thinkers (although later medieval intellectuals would accuse him of ascribing his translated works to himself as original texts, thus damaging his reputation during the later Middle Ages). One tradition about Constantine appears in a series of biographies produced at Monte Cassino, the monastery where Constantine lived, worked, and died sometime before 1098/99. The earliest such account, which appears in the *Chronica monasterii Casinensis* (Chronicle of Monte Cassino), was likely written by a monk named Guido only a few years after Constantine's death. The latest biography in this tradition comes from the compendium of the biographies of famous men by Peter the Deacon (1107–59).[2]

Both the earlier straightforward account and Peter's later embellished biography told of Constantine travelling from his birthplace of Tunis (or Carthage) to Cairo for education (and, according to Peter, even farther, to India and Ethiopia). After many years of study and travel he returned to North Africa where, it is claimed, his considerable learning made him hateful to his compatriots who crafted a plan to kill him. Escaping in secret by boat, he arrived at Salerno in a state of poverty. Eventually, he found patronage and support from both secular and ecclesiastical figures in the region, which fact allowed him to become a monk under Abbot Desiderius of Monte Cassino. There, he translated an extensive list of works into Latin, all pertaining to health and medicine. Living at the Abbey of Monte Cassino until his death around 1098/99, Constantine worked assiduously at translating scientific texts from the Arabic corpus.

A different tradition, written by a twelfth-century physician named Matheus Ferrarius of Salerno, claims that Constantine first travelled to Italy as a merchant and, learning of the paltry state of European science, intentionally sailed back to North Africa seeking books that he could translate to help them.[3] His journey was marred by shipwreck, however, and some of the books he was transporting were lost at sea. It is certainly the case that Salerno was a city actively involved in trade with the Muslim world, as were the nearby ports of Naples, Amalfi, and Gaeta, and so the arrival of a merchant

---

2 Peter the Deacon, *De viris illustribus* 23, in *Monte Cassino in the Middle Ages*, ed. Herbert Bloch, 3 vols. (Cambridge, MA: Harvard University Press, 1986), appendix IV: 1:127–34.

3 Francis Newton, "Arabic Medicine in Europe," in *Mediterranean Passages: Readings from Dido to Derrida*, ed. Miriam Cooke, Erdag Goknar, and Grant Parker (Chapel Hill: University of North Carolina, 2008), 116–17. This contains the biography of Constantine written by Matheus Ferrarius of Salerno.

from North Africa makes perfect sense. In this version of events, Constantine's reception in the city is conditioned by the already-advanced state of medical knowledge and interest among the educated and the elite there. Constantine and a local man then conversed about medicines and diagnostic techniques, through the mediation of enslaved Muslims acting as translators. The picture of Salerno presented in this text is that of a bustling multi-cultural port city with an active intellectual culture, one in which an educated immigrant from North Africa could find a welcome reception and local translators between Arabic and Latin or Romance.

A third narrative, which is an outlier, claims that Constantine fled to Italy not from North Africa but from al-Andalus (Spain). In this later story, preserved only in a thirteenth-century text from England, he escaped from Cordoba because he misdiagnosed the ruler, and made his way to Italy via enslavement. While this version of his life and migration differs significantly from the other two—and most likely from reality—it does highlight similar themes, including Constantine's extensive education, his flight from a hostile homeland, and his welcome reception at Salerno, thanks perhaps in part to the patronage of local elites. It also highlights many of the common reasons we find for individual emigration and flight: falling from favour with a local ruler or patron, fear of danger for personal and professional reasons, and being relocated against one's will as a slave.

Constantine's North African origin is most likely to have been the true story, for several reasons. One is the fact that Constantine refers to himself as "the African," rather than as an Andalusi (Iberian). His own identity as a native of Africa was important enough, either personally or as a marker of his authority as an expert on texts from the Islamic world, for him to insist on its inclusion in his "signature." The second factor is that the pre-existing patterns of travel, trade, and communication linked southern Italy most strongly with North Africa. Whether directly or mediated by ports in Sicily, ships regularly sailed between southern Italy and the many ports along the northern shores of Africa. Thirdly, a high proportion of the Arabic-Islamic texts that Constantine translated were written by authors who worked in North Africa. Despite the biographical tradition stating that Constantine travelled far and wide collecting materials, it is likely that he could have found them all in the city of Qayrawan (modern Kairouan, Tunisia).

Constantine's migration, wherever he came from, took him to the southern Italian city of Salerno, where a program of collecting, editing, and study of medical texts (from late antique and ancient sources, in Greek and Latin) was already underway. But Muslim scholars and scientists had access to more texts translated from ancient Greek than did scholars in western Europe at the time. Arabic-language medical practitioners had also expanded on the ancient sciences, thus forming a rich body of work that the Christian practitioners at Salerno were eager to gain access to through Constantine's transmission and translation work. If, as some of the biographical sources suggest, Constantine was already learned in medical science, he may have specifically chosen Salerno as an ideal locale for his migration because his expertise would be most welcomed there. His translation program also helped spur greater interest in medical learning in Salerno, which later came to be known for its medical school (the Schola Medica Salernitana).

Contemporary events, too, suggest the likelihood of a migration from Tunisia. The late eleventh century was a time of incredible upheaval in North Africa. The Aghlabid Emirate, which had controlled both North Africa and Sicily from its capital at Qayrawan, and paid at least nominal allegiance to the Sunni caliphs at Baghdad, had been replaced in 972 by the Zirid dynasty, governing in the name of the Shi'ite Fatimid caliphs in Cairo. But in 1048 the Zirids attempted to throw off Fatimid rule and to reestablish a connection to the Sunni caliphate. Traditional histories relate that the Fatimid response was to unleash upon Zirid territory savage attacks by Bedouin tribes. Referred to as the Hilalian invasions, these raids may in fact have taken place for other reasons than Fatimid direction, but they were certainly part of larger trends that led to the marginalization, disorder, and diminishment of the Zirid state.

Agricultural destruction, in large part due to environmental causes, and large-scale famine also contributed to the collapse of centralized Zirid power in Ifriqiya. They lost control of Qayrawan and moved to the coastal port city of Mahdia, which they used as their capital from 1057 until it was taken by the Norman rulers of Sicily in 1148. The population of North Africa in the second half of the eleventh century was thus harassed by invaders, stricken by famine and disease, and living under a regime that was increasingly destabilized and impoverished. In such an environment, scholarship and artistic patronage was at risk of drying up completely, not to mention the threats to personal safety these developments represented.

Italy, likewise, was experiencing upheaval, but it may have appeared to Constantine and others like him as a safer and more secure place to live and work. It is estimated that Constantine arrived in Salerno around 1077, the year that the city was subjugated by the Norman warlord Robert Guiscard. He and members of his extended family had been scooping up cities and strongholds across southern Italy—some Lombard territories, others in the hands of local Latin rulers, and still others under nominal Byzantine control—and in 1061 one member of the family, known as Count Roger, had begun the conquest of Muslim Sicily. That undertaking would extend over several decades, but by 1077 it was clear that the region was undergoing major transformations: Sicily's capital (Palermo) and most important southern port (Mazara) were both under Norman control (since 1072), which altered but did not end the patterns of shipping and communications between the island and the African coastline. By 1091, the island and the Italian mainland territories were completely under Norman control and in 1130 Roger II proclaimed both regions to be one kingdom, with its capital at Palermo. In the 1140s, Roger attacked Muslim port cities of North Africa in an attempt to expand his Mediterranean kingdom.

Constantine's life thus coincided not only with tremendous religio-political changes in the Mediterranean, but also with several of the most important intellectual movements of the early medieval world. Contrary to Peter the Deacon's assertion that Constantine's extensive education made his community in North Africa angry at him, Qayrawan had been a centre of learning and scholarly production before the collapse of the Zirid state and the move of their capital to Mahdia. This was in keeping with larger traditions within the Islamic world, where patronage of scholars and translation of ancient texts from Greek into Arabic was a key part of elite culture.

So although Constantine fled from an unstable political and economic situation in his homeland, it is unlikely that Peter the Deacon was right that his high educational status made him unwelcome there. As with most emiral courts across the Muslim world, patronage of artists, poets, and intellectuals was a key part of the activities of rulers and social elites of North Africa. As we will see below, North Africa was the place to which numerous Muslim scholars fled in the wake of the Christian conquests of Muslim Sicily, as did Jewish merchants who had been based in Sicily before the Norman advent. Many of these Islamic scholars and Jewish merchants found homes and careers in North Africa, while many others travelled from there to courts and schools in the central Islamic lands. And Constantine brought not only his expertise in medical science and the Arabic language with him to Italy, he also carried important books. For that to have been the case, these books must have been readily available to him in Ifriqiya despite the political and economic turmoil.

The Islamic world had long focused on the development of science and scholarship in a range of subjects, both by means of translation from ancient Greek texts and the production of new knowledge. The centuries corresponding to the European Middle Ages, especially the early period, were ones of vibrant intellectual activity across the broad Islamicate world. Across the eleventh and twelfth centuries, Latin thinkers gained access to many ancient texts and ideas by means of translations from Arabic into Latin. This translation movement was aided by Christian conquests of Muslim places, such as Sicily and Spain, but it also took place via population movements and immigration, such as Constantine's. The life and migration of Constantine the African to Salerno, crossing as it did intellectual borders as well as religious and cultural ones, highlights the power of migration to carry trends, technologies, and information to new places.

Chapter 5

Jewish Refugees from the Norman Invasion

ELEVENTH-CENTURY SICILY

Since many medieval migrations were spurred by territorial conquests—especially ones that resulted in significant changes to a region's governance and its dominant religion, language, and culture—the eleventh and twelfth centuries saw significant demographic transformations in the lands surrounding the Mediterranean Sea. The Norman invasion of Muslim Sicily was just one example of the large-scale movements of Christian polities into Muslim lands of the region during these centuries. The Spanish "reconquista" was the progressive southward advance of Christian kingdoms into the Muslim states of the Iberian peninsula, and the crusades, likewise, represent Christian incursions into Muslim spaces and the shifting balance of power in the greater Mediterranean area. These political changes were incredibly significant for broader history, but we should also keep in mind the human aspect of such conquests—they often brought violence, dislocation, death, and significant changes in living conditions, religion, language, and culture for local populations.

Once again, taking a closer look at migration patterns to and from Sicily allows us to see these personal elements in action. Many Sicilian Jews—who, much like the Greek Christian communities in Muslim Sicily, viewed the arrival of the Latin Christian Normans with alarm—decided to migrate away from the island rather than remain under Latin rule. Sicily's Jewish population included both established communities, who had lived on the island since at least the fourth century, and newer arrivals. The latter were members of the highly mobile merchant families whom historians know from a cache of letters and documents called the Cairo Geniza. Many people from the Geniza community of Jews lived only temporarily in Sicily, with other parts of their extended families living in Fustat (Old Cairo) or various cities in North Africa. Several letters written to and from Geniza merchants detail the violence and disruption attendant upon the Norman invasion of the island and its surrounding waters. It is also through these letters that we find some of the most detailed personal accounts of cross-Mediterranean migration in action.

For instance, one Sicilian Jew who had fled from the island to Tyre (in the eastern Mediterranean), wrote a letter to his relative in Fustat with details of the violence and disorder that spurred his migration. He mentioned rampant famine and resultant illness among the population, looting and the plundering of warehouses full of goods, and a sharp increase in prices in Sicily, especially for food.[1] He and his family had been residents of Palermo, the capital of Muslim Sicily, which was captured in 1072 by the Norman invaders. He described the situation: "We witnessed events which I should have gladly done without, namely bloodshed. We trod on corpses as if it were common ground. (There raged) a heavy epidemic" (Simonsohn, 279). He then detailed the rising prices for food, a break-in at one of his warehouses and the theft of his goods, the decline of real estate prices which impacted the value of a house and some orchards that he owned, and the death of his father after a depression that resulted from these financial losses. Despite these economic, personal, and social disasters, he and his surviving family members had enough resources to be able to escape to the eastern Mediterranean. But they were not yet fully settled in their life there: the author calls Tyre "a strange town and I do not know where to turn" (Simonsohn, 279).

I Cambridge, TS 13J13.27; trans. Simonsohn, *The Jews in Sicily*, vol. 1, *383–1300* [hereafter Simonsohn], 278–81 (doc. 131). See also Goitein, *A Mediterranean Society*, 1:122.

Another letter-writer, who was based in North Africa but conveyed the news coming out of Sicily, told similar stories of disaster and emigration. He informed his correspondent that "the situation deteriorates constantly, and everyone is terribly disturbed about the progress of the enemy who has already conquered most of the island [...]. Twelve families of our coreligionists have been taken captive, and countless numbers of Muslims."[2] It was thus not only the risk of death or financial collapse that the Muslims and Jews of Sicily feared from the Christian invasion, but also capture and, possibly, enslavement.

Instead of remaining in Sicily under such dangerous and costly conditions, we have evidence that many people who could leave did so. Many Jews in Sicily took advantage of their connections with Jewish communities in Egypt and North Africa to find new homes safely away from the violence and economic disruption on Sicily. Likewise, many Muslims must have escaped the island, as we will see in the discussion of Muslim scholars below. Unlike the Muslim population, however, the Jewish community's experiences of emigration are well documented by the letters of the Geniza cache. These personal letters to and from members of extended social networks, business partnerships, and family groups demonstrate the disastrous impact of conquest and attempts to migrate to safety.

Unlike the letter-writer above, who fled to the eastern Mediterranean, most of these letters indicate flight to Egypt and North Africa. These were common choices because of long-standing connections between the Jewish communities there and the one in Sicily. A Geniza letter written sometime in the late 1060s, for example, noted that many of the island's inhabitants were seeking to escape to Africa because of the Norman victories in Sicily and the violence of the invasion: "The news from Sicily is bad and deplorable, because

---

2 St. Petersburg, Institute Narodov Azii, D–55, n. 13; S. D. Goitein, *Letters of Medieval Jewish Traders* (Princeton: Princeton University Press, 1973) [hereafter *Letters*], 163–68 (no. 33).

the enemy captured the island [...]. People are leaving for the African mainland" (Simonsohn, 366).[3]

The "African mainland" could indicate North Africa, but several letters written from Egypt show that many ships full of refugees were also arriving there. For example, one letter written by a merchant named Isma'il bin Farah claimed that ten ships docked in Alexandria with refugees from Sicily aboard.[4] Each ship was carrying five hundred passengers—a possible exaggeration meant to convey the magnitude of this flight from disaster in Sicily. Isma'il wrote a second letter about Jewish migration away from Sicily during the turbulent late eleventh century; from his perspective it appeared to be a mass departure heading in many directions at once.[5] He informed his son that a ship full of Sicilians had arrived in Alexandria from Palermo, while a group from the Maghrib (modern Morocco) had at the same time sailed to Egypt via Mazara, an active port city on the southwestern shore of Sicily. That is, from his vantage point in Egypt, he could see multiple shiploads full of refugees arriving from different points of origin all at once.

The middle of the eleventh century was not only politically turbulent in Sicily but was similarly troubled in North Africa. A combination of environmental and military disasters brought much of the North African population to famine, and the related market disruptions, shipment delays, and out-of-control prices are evident throughout the texts from this period. The political collapse of the Zirid capital at Qayrawan, and the emiral court's retreat to the coastal city of Mahdia, meant that people there were exposed to violence and instability; many lost their homes and livelihoods. Some people would have been unable to migrate away from such conditions, but several Geniza letters demonstrate that others did—even though in many cases they fled to an equally unstable situation in Sicily.

---

3 Mosseri Coll. II, 128 (L 130)2; Simonsohn, 365–68 (doc. 158).

4 New York, Theol. Sem., Adler Coll. 2727.38; Simonsohn, 194–95 (doc. 100).

5 Cambridge, TS 10J20.12; Simonsohn, 195–98 (doc. 101).

For example, another of Isma'il's letters detailed the story of his brother Sulayman, who moved to Sicily even while many others were departing the island. His was a tale of great suffering: Sulayman and his family had long sought to escape from the fallen Ifriqiyan capital of Qayrawan but each of their attempts to flee to the coast was obstructed. Isma'il wrote that Sulayman seemed near death by the time he finally escaped, "for during eight months they tried to leave the city for Susa, but were unable to do so. Finally, a group of Muslims and among them some [Jews?] left the city, but the Arabs killed them, cutting their stomachs open and saying 'You have swallowed dinars.'"[6] In like fashion, he writes, some of their Jewish associates had also been killed. Finally making it to the port city of Susa, Sulayman and his family found circumstances no better: an uprising there resulted in the plundering of shops and warehouses, and the burning of citadels: "That my brother escaped safely via Susa is a miracle" (*Letters*, 155). The family sought refuge in Mazara, Sicily, where Sulayman was able to help manage the family's business affairs.

A later letter from Isma'il, however, shows that life in Sicily was not much better for Sulayman and his family. He had received a letter from his brother in which "he writes that he is in a terrible state. Others write the same. In short: he who had anything went away, and he who had something belonging to someone else consumed it. Even a case of cannibalism has been reported" (Simonsohn, 197). Isma'il also related that his sister and her daughters had moved to Mahdia, along with twenty-three other families in dire need ("destitute and naked"), but it is not specified where they migrated from. These crossed paths of migration represent the search for safety and prosperity at a time when nowhere in the central Mediterranean seemed to offer much of either.

Similarly, two Geniza letters by Salama bin Musa Safaqusi ("the Sfaxian," indicating his connection with the North African seaport of Sfax) from the mid-eleventh century pro-

---

6 London, BM Or. 5542.9; *Letters*, 153–58 (no. 31); Simonsohn, 191–93 (doc. 99).

vide another window into the conditions in North Africa that inspired some people to migrate to Sicily.[7] Dated circa 1064, this letter was written by a North African merchant to his business partner based in Egypt, but dispatched from Mazara, Sicily. It describes the harrowing conditions from which he had escaped the year prior in Mahdia, where he had been conducting business but then came into conflict with political authorities and other merchants. His business deals went south, he was denounced to the authorities for hiding goods, and he encountered the military movements of the sultan's army against other Ifriqiyan rulers. So Salama fled to Mazara; once in Sicily, he felt unable to return to North Africa because of political violence and broken relationships. So he purchased a house in Mazara and sent for his family to join him from Sfax. Even though the Norman invaders had already taken some Sicilian towns in the northeast of the island, the southwestern region was still thought safe enough that it was considered preferable to the dangers to be found in North Africa.

Through personal letters like these, we can glimpse groups of migrants simultaneously fleeing to Sicily from North Africa, away from Sicily to North Africa and Egypt, and away from North Africa and the Maghrib toward Egypt. There was no one single path that all migrants followed. In this time of political unrest, economic crisis, and violence in many regions, even different members of the same family moved in different directions at once, relying on their widespread networks of friends, family, and business associates to seek refuge and safer conditions. Different branches of the same family might be living far apart and moving in different directions, waiting to hear news of loved ones through letters that arrived on the same ships as masses of refugees.

---

7 Philadelphia, Dropsie College 389; Simonsohn, 332–44 (doc. 151); and Philadelphia, Dropsie College 414; Simonsohn, 345–46 (doc. 152). Transcription and translation in Moshe Gil, "The Jews in Sicily under Muslim Rule, in the Light of the Geniza Documents," in *Italia judaica* (Rome: Ministero per i beni culturali e ambientali, 1983), 87–134. See also Goitein, *A Mediterranean Society*, 1:245; 2:68, 2:162, 2:294.

And many of these families moved more than once—seeking safety but often finding only more upheaval. Thus even though migration within and across the central Mediterranean during the eleventh century presented numerous options for destinations, none assured the refugees a safe and stable life in a new land. Like migrants from the earlier period, violence and regime change in one place was often matched by that in other regions, meaning that it could be difficult to find a safe new home. And, like the earlier refugees fleeing regime change and destruction of property, many Jews and Muslims who relocated in the eleventh and twelfth centuries engaged in multi-stage migrations. Seeking safety in one place, they might find further turmoil that led them to migrate again if they could do so. For medieval people, migration was clearly a difficult and costly process that could easily end in disaster or further difficulty.

Chapter 6

Merchants

ELEVENTH AND TWELFTH-CENTURY MEDITERRANEAN

The Geniza community included highly mobile merchants who, as we have seen, could use their personal and professional contacts to seek refuge from invading forces. But these letters show that migration among this community had in fact begun prior to the Norman conquest of Sicily and the collapse of Zirid power in Ifriqiya. Indeed, not all migrations were spurred by events like regime change, conquest, or religious persecution—sometimes they were based on pragmatic business decisions like where the best deals could be made or where a new trade could be established after a setback. And migrants followed paths that were also traced by merchants, pilgrims, diplomats, and scholars. Travel across the sea was dependent upon locating a ship going to and from particular ports, along well-sailed sealanes in sight of the shorelines. So it comes as no surprise that many of the ships and shipping lanes on which migrants sailed were the same ones that transported merchandise, pilgrims, political officials, envoys, and scholars. Individuals who were already familiar with ships, ports, and foreign cities might find the process of migration a little easier than those who were not.

The business trips mentioned in the Geniza letters—spanning the Mediterranean Sea and Indian Ocean regions—show clearly that the Jews who belonged to this widespread community moved from place to place with relative ease, even though relocation to a new place often entailed some level of hardship. But it was not only Jewish merchants who could use their business networks or knowledge of foreign lands as resources for migration—merchants from all cultures were known to have moved regularly across the medieval world, sometimes temporarily and sometimes permanently. Colonies of merchants established in foreign entrepôts were key players in long-distance trade, but they also facilitated cultural exchange—such as the spread of Islam along the shores of the Indian Ocean and the China Seas. We know, for example, that colonies of foreign traders—many from the Arabic- and Persian-speaking worlds—were established in Chinese port cities like Guangzhou (Canton) from as early as the eighth century.

Many Geniza letters show migration as a commonplace among these mercantile communities—for instance, when detailing the conflicts between family members or business partners who lived far apart. The letters testify to the fact that when members of extended families lived at a distance from each other, family relations could at times be difficult. One example of a family whose members lived in different places is found in the record of a court case about a property disagreement between two brothers, one of whom lived in Qayrawan while the other resided in Palermo.[1] The disputed land was in Palermo, where one of the brothers, his wife, and his wife's brothers lived. The Palermitan brother, called Abu Zikri, operated a shop owned by his brother Samuel, who was at that time living in Qayrawan, although the document does not specify why or for how long he had been living in North Africa. This type of arrangement, in which close family members lived in different places around the Mediterranean basin, seems to have been fairly common among the Geniza community. The only reason we know of this case is that the distant brothers were fighting over the arrangement and left a record of the dispute, not because of a dramatic story of migration like those in the previous chapter.

---

1 Paris, Alliance Israelite Universelle, VII D–108; Simonsohn, doc. 75.

Another example is that of a letter written by a widow in the Sicilian town of Ragusa whose son lived in Fustat, Egypt. Her letter asked him to return to Sicily to comfort her before her death, perhaps suggesting that he had been gone from the island for a long time.[2] These documents do not provide direct evidence for when, why, or how the various family members migrated—only that some people within a family might migrate while others remained in the place of origin, or that close family members might migrate together but end up in different places. This particular letter also allows us to glimpse the emotional pain of a mother whose son had emigrated, and the impact that his absence had on her.

An example of an extended family who emigrated together but wound up living in different places is found in a series of letters between the families of two brothers-in-law who had left Spain together. Their families ended up in different locations further east in the Mediterranean—one in Egypt and the other in either Sicily or North Africa.[3] Evidence suggests that their migrations took place in the first half of the eleventh century, prior to the arrival of the Normans. It was a period of turmoil in other regions, however, including al-Andalus (Muslim Spain), where their families had originated; at that time, Sicily appeared to be a safer place. The group of family letters, which contain a mix of personal news and business dealings, indicate that the Iberian family was spread widely across the central and eastern Mediterranean: in addition to members in Egypt and either Sicily or North Africa, one of the men residing in Egypt had relocated his wife and children to Jerusalem. Presumably, he intended to join them when finances allowed. Although he and his family had, at the time of these letters, settled in various places on a perhaps temporary basis, their departure from Spain was permanent: after the deaths of the two brothers-in-law, cor-

---

2 New York, Theol. Sem., Adler Coll. 3792.4; Simonsohn, doc. 132.

3 Cambridge, TS 20.127; *Letters*, 111–20 (no. 22). Goitein, *A Mediterranean Society*, 1:376 and 1:178.

respondence continued between their sons, none of whom had returned to Spain.

The relative ease with which these Jewish individuals and families could migrate across the Mediterranean is related to the mercantile activities and mobility of this community. They transported loads of commodities between the markets of Sicily, Egypt, and North Africa, taking their goods to wherever the highest prices were to be found. Among the most valuable commodities mentioned were various spices, dyestuffs, silk material and sewn clothing, flax, cotton, other textiles, and food products. Many letters contain references to market fluctuations resulting from political and military upheavals in various regions; many letter-writers urged the addressee to bring his goods somewhere to take advantage of good prices. Other letters contain admonitions that the recipient take his goods to some other place, since the rumor was that market demand was greater there. One letter states: "This year, the price of flax was very low in al-Mahdiyya [Mahdia] and in Sicily. However, the spices sold well because of their rarity."[4] Letters also detail business dealings in many products, with many partners, in many directions all at once. A single merchant might be in partnership with multiple others located throughout the Mediterranean world, sending and receiving various goods at many ports, all with an eye to maximizing profit. This broad familiarity with many places could facilitate the acquisition of a new home when necessary, but also regularly produced a number of business-related hassles.

Commerce could thus be a source both of opportunity and of disaster. Financial affairs provided merchants with paths for migration, but could also be the reason that they sought to migrate in the first place. For instance, one Geniza letter written prior to the Norman invasion suggests that Jewish migration away from Muslim Sicily had been increasing because of financial pressures, even before the onset of wartime violence and regime change. This letter from Palermo's Jewish community, written to a Jewish leader in Jerusalem,

---

4 Cambridge, TS 16.163; *Letters*, 128–34 (no. 25).

begs forgiveness for the lack of a monetary donation accompanying the letter.[5] Sicily's Jews, the author writes, had been facing a dire financial threat in the form of an increased *jizya*, the head tax that Muslim authorities exacted upon members of religious minority communities across the Islamicate world. This was the cause of both impoverishment for Sicily's Jews and the emigration of many of them. The letter-writer only tells us that they moved "overseas," not their specific routes or destinations. Even without details, however, we might presume that these Jews had relocated to one of the cities in North Africa or Egypt that were regularly in close communication and connection with Sicily.

Other merchants migrated because they perceived greater opportunities for success abroad. Just as Geniza merchants went where good prices and good deals could be found, so too did the merchants from the Latin Christian world who became increasingly dominant in the later medieval Mediterranean economy. In the early medieval period, merchants from southern Italian cities like Amalfi and Salerno had been major agents of cross-cultural commercial exchange in the Mediterranean. Around the twelfth century, however, we see a shift in economic power toward northern cities like Genoa and Pisa; Venetians had long dominated the eastern Mediterranean and their power only increased during and after the crusades.

One example of traders migrating to take advantage of this northward shift is found in the story of a merchant family from Salerno, Solomon and his wife Eliadar, who migrated to Genoa sometime in mid-twelfth century.[6] There, the husband and wife—both together and independently—engaged in business deals that involved merchants and goods from every part of the Mediterranean. Solomon himself travelled widely: to Alexandria, Cairo, Sicily, Mallorca, and Spain; his

---

5 New York, Theol. Sem., Adler Coll. 4009.4; Simonsohn, doc. 39.

6 David Abulafia, *The Great Sea*, 301–3; and Abulafia, *The Two Italies*, 237–54. Abulafia finds no evidence that Solomon and Eliadar, despite their names, were Jews.

business deals also involved Byzantium and southern France and North Africa. Eliadar oversaw trade deals both at home in Genoa and overseas, which involved southern France and Sicily. Not all of their business went perfectly smoothly—involvement in political affairs caused them significant financial setbacks—but their decision to move to Genoa clearly paid off.

The Venetians were aided in their rise to economic power in the eastern Mediterranean by their establishment of merchant colonies in Constantinople and nearby ports. A Venetian population in Constantinople existed from the early Middle Ages; by 1082 it was granted governing autonomy over its own quarter of the city. Constantinople also had communities of Muslim and Jewish traders and, by the end of the Middle Ages, ones of Genoese, Germans, French, and other European traders. But the Venetian quarter in Constantinople was always the most prominent. But in 1171 the Venetians lost favour with the emperor, who expelled them violently. At that time, many of the merchants who had lived and done business there were forced to flee—either back to Venice or to other trading outposts in the Mediterranean. One example was the merchant Romano Mairano, who returned to Venice after the political trouble in Constantinople, where he had been living as a trader for we do not know how long. His commercial connections allowed him to weather this storm of financial loss and exile. He continued to trade and travel throughout the eastern Mediterranean for about fifteen years, until the next emperor reversed the anti-Venetian policy and Romano returned to Constantinople. The Venetians recovered their standing and, after the Fourth Crusade, developed an economic empire in the eastern Mediterranean. By the time of the Ottoman takeover, the Venetian colony in the city was of considerable size and power, composed of a wide range of people beyond simply traders and ambassadors.

Constantinople, however, was not the only Mediterranean city containing outposts of foreign traders living there on a permanent or semi-permanent basis. Venetians had long maintained colonies in other Byzantine towns, and they and other Italians established new ones in ports along the

Levantine coast that were conquered during the crusades. As Italian mercantile cities developed naval fleets, they came to be important players in transporting soldiers and supply missions to crusader-held territories in the Levant, and in the naval battles that assisted crusading forces in the capture of ports such as Tyre and Acre. The Genoese, Pisans, and Venetians, in particular, were granted tax exemptions and autonomous control over portions of the port cities in exchange for these assistances. Just as with other long-term migrants to the crusader lands, where new fortunes could be made, these Italian outposts came to be home to foreigners living and working abroad.

And it was not only Italians who lived in foreign enclaves in Mediterranean cities. Other trading ports along the shores of the Mediterranean contained vast quarters for foreign merchants that might be composed of temporary and more permanent residents. In highly active mercantile cities, there would be different quarters of, for example, Genoese, Pisans, Catalans, and French. Each quarter was filled with the institutions and cultural elements of the home city—taverns, churches or mosques, inns, ovens, brothels, markets, warehouses, cemeteries—with a local governor called a consul. In other words, these were not hostels for temporary visits, but were developing into long-term foreign enclaves. Such merchant colonies abroad provided individuals with opportunities to migrate for profit or to escape disaster, just as the Geniza Jews used their widespread networks to seek new homes abroad after personal, professional, or political trouble threatened their livelihoods at home. Thus we see that Mediterranean people with a high degree of mobility, like merchants and, as we will see below, Muslim scholars, were able to take advantage of their interpersonal networks to emigrate when necessary. The pathways of migration were woven into the fabric of medieval travel more broadly.

Chapter 7

Imam al-Mazari and Other Muslim Scholars

TWELFTH-CENTURY SICILY AND NORTH AFRICA

While the Geniza evidence allows us to see Jewish migration in action, other population groups who moved to or from Sicily at this time are less visible. We know, for example, that many Muslim Sicilians fled the oncoming Christian invaders, but we rarely find evidence of their moves until long after the fact. Like merchants who migrated because they were already regular travellers, many of the Muslim emigrants we know of were scholars who used their intellectual networks to find new patronage when circumstances dictated. Some of the most mobile of medieval people were Muslim scholars, known collectively as 'ulama', who regularly travelled across the expanse of the Islamicate world in order to teach, study, and learn together. Gathering in madrasas (schools), mosques, and at princely courts, these scholars—who were masters of philosophy, biography, poetry, theology, law, and a variety of sciences—would share books, learn from other masters, and debate ideas. Many Muslim intellectuals moved several times over the course of their careers, seeking both knowledge and patronage. Due to the established networks by which these educated elite moved around the Mediterranean world and beyond, many were also able to permanently relocate with their families in the wake of military conquest, political crisis, or loss of patronage. Numerous examples of intellectuals from Muslim Sicily, for example, only show up in the textual sources because they did just that: they fled the approach of Latin Christian conquerors in Sicily and relocated in Muslim cities or courts in al-Andalus, Egypt, or North Africa.

The conquering Normans were Latin Christians but made no pronouncements about the faith of their subjects nor issued a requirement for conversion, at least not explicitly. But the predominantly Muslim population of the island would have understood that they had a religious obligation to seek a safe home abroad rather than stay in a land governed by non-Muslims. Unlike Jews, who had no scriptural edict guiding their choices about whether to stay in a hostile place or to leave it (although, as we will see below, some thinkers and immigrants like Maimonides advocated in favour of migration under such circumstances), Muslims were guided by a Qur'anic injunction against dwelling in territories ruled by non-Muslims. Based on a series of verses suggesting that there was neither earthly virtue nor eternal reward for those living under oppression, and that God's earth was spacious enough for believers to find homes in territories under Muslim political control, Islamic legal scholars developed what is known as the doctrine of emigration (*hijra*)—the "obligation to emigrate."[1]

The juridical reasoning behind this obligation focused on the need for a support structure in which individual Muslim believers could best carry out the tenets of their faith. The idea was that the full practice of Islam depended upon a community of Muslims and proper Islamic leadership in order to conduct the basic rituals and practices of their faith, including those surrounding birth, death, foodways, and education in religious traditions. Local community judges were needed to settle disputes and answer questions about specific issues not found in the Qur'an, and legitimate political authority was necessary to oversee it all. These practical needs were supplemented by the belief that Muslims, as adherents to the highest religious truth, should not in any way be subjected to the authority of non-Muslim rulers. Thus the injunction was

---

1 Qur'an Sura 4:97–100, Sura 8:70–4, Sura 16:110, and Sura 29:56.

that Muslims whose territories were conquered by non-Muslims should migrate to the lands of Islam.

However, the reality of many people's lives meant that they either could not or chose not to leave their homes and livelihoods in order to seek an uncertain future in an unknown land. Establishing a stable life in a new place was often quite a long and difficult process, as we have seen, and required financial resources that were beyond the reach of many people. Others might have found themselves on the wrong side of a newly drawn border without enough advance warning to enable them to flee. And medieval sources make it clear that conquests sometimes could be quickly reversed, so some people whose land was under attack might have waited to see what would happen in the end and thereby lost their chance to leave. Whatever the reason, we know that many Muslims remained in Mediterranean territories taken by Christian conquerors in the mid- to late-eleventh century. This fact spurred some Islamic legal experts to consider the question of what to do about Muslims who contravened the obligation to emigrate by persisting as minority communities in Christian lands.

One such legal expert was a man known as Imam al-Mazari (d. 1141), one of the chief judges in Ifriqiya. It is evident from his name that al-Mazari's ancestors had come from Sicily (specifically, the southwestern port of Mazara) at some point, although we do not know precisely when. It is not clear whether the jurist himself was born in Sicily or in North Africa, before or after the family's migration. We also do not know with certainty the reason for his family's migration to North Africa: it might well have been the Norman invasion that prompted their move; the timeline makes this a strong possibility. This was certainly the case for many Muslim scholars and experts whose biographies explicitly state that they or their families fled the oncoming Christian forces.

An example of a scholar who is known to have fled the Norman invasion was the Sicilian-born scholar Ibn al-Qatta' (1041–1121/22). His youth was spent studying with master scholars in Muslim Sicily, learning the traditions of Arabic literature and scholarship. We have a brief account of his life and migrations contained in a North African compilation of biographies of important scholars.[2] It specifies that he departed from the island when it had become clear that the Christians were on the verge of controlling the entire island. This might refer to the year 1072, a pivotal moment for the Christian conquest. In that year the Normans gained control of both the capital city of Palermo and Mazara, the island's most significant southern port. In 1072, Ibn al-Qatta' was about thirty years old and a well-established member of local intellectual circles, likely meaning that he had enough connections abroad to help him find a patron. Moving first to al-Andalus, probably in search of patronage at the court of a Muslim ruler, he later ended up in Egypt where he worked until his death.

Similar paths of migration from the besieged island to Muslim Spain and thence to Egypt or Tunisia were taken by a number of Sicilian poets working in the Arabic literary tradition. The most famous of these is also Sicily's best-known intellectual from the Muslim period, the poet known as Ibn Hamdis (1055–1132). In 1078, he left Sicily and travelled westward, seeking patronage at the court of the ruler of the small kingdom of Muslim Seville, al-Mu'tamid (r. 1069–91). The arrangement was beneficial to them both: the petty king gained a lustre of legitimacy by filling his court with intellectuals and artists, and the poet gained a safe home and financial support.

Even though we have a significant corpus of poetry by Ibn Hamdis, a number of questions about his life and migration remained unanswered.[3] A native of Syracuse, Ibn Hamdis

---

2 Ibn Khallikān, *Wafayāt al-aʿyān wa-anbaʾ abnaʾ al-zamān*, ed. Ihsān ʿAbbās, 8 vols. (Beirut: Dār al-Thaqāfa, 1968–77): 3:322–24.

3 Many of Ibn Hamdis's poems are translated in William Granara, "Ibn Ḥamdīs and the Poetry of Nostalgia," in *The Literature of al-Andalus*, ed. Maria Rosa Menocal, Raymond P. Scheindlin, and Michael Sells (Cambridge: Cambridge University Press, 2000), 388–403.

may initially have departed from his homeland for professional reasons, rather than explicitly because of the Norman invasion. Syracuse did not fall to Norman forces until 1086, eight years after Ibn Hamdis left the island. It may be that he had gone abroad seeking patronage and was then prevented from returning home after the conquest of his city. Or, perhaps he was able to envision the ultimate fall of Sicily to the Normans, given that by the late 1070s nearly all of the island's major cities and ports were under Norman control. He may have feared that Syracuse would not last long as an independent Muslim city-state, as in fact it did not.

Migration, and its irreversibility, is a persistent theme in Ibn Hamdis's poetic corpus. Many of his verses express great longing for his lost homeland, which he (rightly) feared he would never see again. For example: "I remember Sicily, as agony stirs in my soul all remembrances of her./An abode for the pleasures of my youth, now vacated, once inhabited by the noblest of people./For I have been banished from paradise, and I long to tell you its story" (Granara, 397). In another poem, he relates the personal grief brought on by his exile: "I am a man resigned to a sorrow that has left a scar in his heart./I always thought my homeland would return to its people, but such thinking was wrong, and I am now in despair" (Granara, 398). The poet linked his own personal story with the history of territorial losses for Islam as a whole to create heart-rending verses of loss and longing.

After thirteen years of composing poetry at the court in Seville, that state was itself conquered and Ibn Hamdis was forced to migrate again. The small Islamic kingdoms of post-Umayyad Iberia were conquered in the mid-eleventh century by the Almoravids, an Indigenous tribal confederation from North Africa. The ruler of Seville, al-Mu'tamid, was deposed and taken into captivity, and Ibn Hamdis relocated again, this time to the court of Tamim ibn al-Mu'izz (d. 1108), the Zirid emir of Mahdia, in North Africa. Tamim was possibly in the best position to try to regain Sicily from the Normans, and Ibn Hamdis may have hoped, or even lobbied, for this outcome, although in vain. Many of his poems make reference to his desire for a future reversal of the Christian conquest: "If my country were free, I would go to it with a resolve that considers journeying to it an absolute necessity./But my country, how can I release it from captivity, while it sits in the clutches of the usurping infidels?" (Granara, 400). In fact, Zirid troops had aided Sicilian resistance to the Norman conquest in the 1070s, but those efforts were brief and unsuccessful. By the time Ibn Hamdis arrived at Mahdia in 1091, the entire island was under Norman control, and he and other Sicilian émigrés could do nothing but long for their lost homeland.

Imam al-Mazari's family presumably migrated along a similar path, although we do not know whether they fled first to somewhere like al-Andalus, or directly to North Africa. What is clear is that they retained their identity as Sicilians even after fifty or more years in North Africa. So too did many of the other scholars who migrated from Sicily to Islamic lands, whom we know from the later medieval collection of scholars' biographies. Many of these intellectuals and their families retained names or nicknames that identified them with Sicily as a whole (such as "the Sicilian") or with a specific place name (like "al-Mazari," from the city of Mazara). Many other people in North Africa likely also maintained names or other identity markers linking them to their Sicilian heritage, but we cannot locate them in the extant sources.

The corpus of al-Mazari's juridical rulings suggests that the Muslims in Sicily continued to be important to him, and perhaps to a local community of Sicilian refugees living near him in North Africa who brought their questions to the judge. He showed concern for the Sicilians by issuing a number of juristic responses about Muslims living in contradiction to the obligation to emigrate. These legal questions would likely have been posed to him from his fellow North Africans, suggesting that there were continued links between them and their friends and family who had stayed behind on the island. Groups of friends and business associates, or members of extended families, on either side of a new boundary appear to have maintained, if not direct communication with each other, then at least a level of concern for those on the other side.

One such legal decision featured al-Mazari wrestling with the very existence of a Muslim community in Christian Sicily: debating whether Muslims should be allowed to remain as minorities in Christian Sicily at all. The question presented to him was specifically about the legitimacy of legal pronouncements from the chief religious judge for the island's Muslim population.[4] The questioner did not know why the judge had remained in Christian Sicily, whether voluntarily or under duress, but we know from other evidence that he owed his official position to the Christian king: the Normans allowed the Muslim minority population to keep its community leaders, but only ones whom they approved and appointed. The questioner wanted to know whether this judge's legal opinions should be considered binding even though he was living in a state of subjection and working for a non-Muslim ruler. Presumably, the basis for the question was the belief that if the judge were determined to be an unfaithful Muslim because he lived in contravention of the obligation to emigrate, then his legal pronouncements would likewise be invalid. And, by extension, the Sicilian Muslim community that he served would be left without proper leadership and thus spiritually endangered.

Imam al-Mazari answered in the affirmative: the judge's rulings were to be obeyed exactly as if he had been appointed by a Muslim ruler rather than a Christian one. He supported this pronouncement with a series of legal justifications, all amounting to the dual desire to trust the judge's reasons for living in Christian Sicily and to protect the integrity of the island's minority Muslim population by recognizing their local community leader as a fit guide to living a proper Muslim life. In other words, al-Mazari recognized that there might be valid reasons for the judge, and by extension the entire community of Sicilian Muslims, to be living in Christian territory and

---

4 Aḥmad ibn Yaḥyā al-Wansharīsī, *al-Miʻyār al-mʻurib wa-al-jāmiʻ al-maghrib ʻan fatāwā ahl Ifrīqiyah wa-al-Andalus wa-al-Maghrib*, ed. Muḥammad Hajjī, 13 vols. (Rabat: Wizārat al-Awqāf wa al-Shu'ūn al-Islāmīyah lil-Mamlakah al-Maghribīyah, 1981–83): 10:107–8.

that they should not be abandoned or ignored by the rest of the Muslim world.

At the same time, al-Mazari warned North Africans against intentionally travelling to Norman Sicily for a variety of reasons, including the possibility that they might be prohibited from leaving and forced to live as subjects of the non-Muslim rulers. From other sources, we know that Muslim scholars, merchants, and pilgrims visited the island and safely left it. In the specific case of Sicily, however, freedom of movement differed for native Muslims and for those who visited the island from abroad. The conquered population, with whom al-Mazari's legal response was concerned, had not been able to flee the island like the North Africa-based scholars. Their families were, by the later twelfth century, even further restricted in their movements and freedoms. This population did not have the same level of financial means as the scholars and pilgrims who arrived in Sicily from abroad, and they were mostly relegated to agricultural labour on the fields of western Sicily. Other accounts make it clear that some of the fears about life for minority Muslim populations were coming true: elite members of the community were feeling pressure to convert to Christianity and were restricted from leaving the island. Whether the North African judge knew these facts or only feared them, he was sure that no one should willingly travel from elsewhere to Sicily lest they not be able to depart.

Despite the restrictions on freedom of movement for Sicily's native Muslims, some foreign Muslim visitors had no problems coming and going freely from the island. In fact, the Norman kings are famous for their patronage of Muslim intellectuals and artisans, attracting scholars to their royal court in the same fashion as Muslim rulers of al-Andalus, North Africa, and elsewhere. The most famous of these scholars is known as al-Idrisi, a geographer and cartographer born in the Maghrib about 1100. Like many of his fellow 'ulama', he travelled extensively for education and study, although not perhaps initially in the geographical sciences. How he came to the attention of the Norman king of Sicily, Roger II (1097–1154), is unclear. But it seems that in about 1138 Roger invited al-Idrisi to his court for the purpose of commissioning a world map and accompanying geographical commentary. After fifteen years of study and collaboration with other scholars under Roger's patronage, al-Idrisi presented to Roger a map engraved on silver (which is no longer extant) and a description of the world, its peoples, and its cultures as it was known to him. The focus of the geographical treatise was Sicily, the island that Roger's father had conquered and which he had declared a new kingdom in 1130. Known usually as the *Book of Roger*, the geographical description of the island gives historians unparalleled information about the island and conceptions of the Mediterranean world at the time, but unfortunately tells us nothing about al-Idrisi's migration, how he felt about his new homeland, or his long absence from the place of his birth.[5]

Like al-Idrisi, other Muslim scholars and poets were invited to the Norman royal court, as we will see further below. But their migration stories are typically not included in their medieval biographies. As elite scholars and artists, patronized by kings and princes, it was not their relocation but their cultural production that mattered most to medieval authors. But even when the act of migration is invisible in our sources, it remained an important factor in cross-cultural transfers of information and technologies, just like we have seen in the cases of Constantine the African and Hadrian and Theodore.

But the accounts of people like Imam al-Mazari and the poet Ibn Hamdis show the more tragic side of migration—the emotional loss and feelings of exile, and the difficulties experienced when some members of a community could migrate away from a conquered land while others could not. Their stories also show us that there were entire communities of people affected by migration whose individual experiences and even their names remain unknown to historians.

---

5 Abū Abd Allāh Muḥammad al-Idrīsī, *Opus geographicum, sive "Liber ad eorum delectationem qui terras peragrare studeant"*, ed. Enrico Cerulli and Francesco Gabrieli et al., 2nd ed., 9 vols. (Naples/Rome: Istituto Universitario Orientale di Napoli/Istituto Italiano per il Medio ed Estremo Oriente, 1970–84).

Chapter 8

Unnamed Sicilian Girl

TWELFTH-CENTURY SICILY

Women's migration experiences are particularly hard to access, due both to the preoccupation of most medieval texts with the lives of named men and to the specific dangers that migration presented to women travelling alone. While we certainly know that women undertook long journeys on their own volition for a variety of reasons, many Christian women who travelled were wealthy pilgrims with an entourage. We also know that Jewish and Muslim women travelled—for pilgrimage, marriage, to visit relatives, and at holiday times—although less frequently than men. The conditions of migration were far more precarious even than those of pilgrimage or other long-distance journeys, however, which may mean that few women would have migrated independently of their family group.

We know, for instance, that the Jewish scholar Moses Maimonides (on whom more below) migrated together with his whole family—including father, mother, brother, and at least two sisters—even though the sources reveal very little about the women of the family and how they might have experienced migration differently than Moses and his brother or father. The difficulties that this family encountered while seeking a settled life in a new land also highlight the vulnerability of migrants, even ones as well positioned as Maimonides' family. Women migrating alone or with young children would have faced even more dangerous challenges. Many women likely would not have chosen to migrate without the surety of a home at the end of their journey.

We can get a glimpse of these issues through the story of an unnamed Sicilian Muslim girl written down by the Muslim traveller Ibn Jubayr. Having spent several months in Christian Norman Sicily (in the winter of 1184–85) on his return home to Granada after pilgrimage to Mecca, Ibn Jubayr related important information about the conditions of life for Muslim minorities in Sicily under King William II. While he was initially impressed by the king's attitude of acceptance toward Muslim courtiers—guards, tailors, cooks, concubines, and others at the king's royal palace who spoke Arabic and practised Islam with, he claimed, the full knowledge of the king—by the end of his time on the island, Ibn Jubayr had come to believe that Norman Christian society was oppressive to the native Muslims. He personally witnessed events and heard second-hand stories about Norman attempts to disenfranchise elite members of the native Muslim population, and what appeared to him to be an effort to force conversion and disintegration of the community. While simultaneously patronizing foreign artists and scholars from the central Islamic lands and surrounding themselves with Muslim art, imagery, and courtiers, the Norman kings had imposed a travel ban on native Muslims and instituted restrictive policies that kept them from practicing their faith and culture to the fullest.

One of the last stories he heard before boarding a ship bound for Granada was of a Sicilian girl seeking a way to leave the island.[1] The girl, unnamed in the text, was being offered by her father as a marriage partner to any of the Spanish Muslim pilgrims who might wish to take her to Granada. Their concern was that she marry into a Muslim family, even if that meant separation from her natal family across the sea. The reason, we are told, is that the father wished to help her escape from the oppressions of life in Christian Sicily and to prevent her conversion to Christianity. We might surmise that she was perhaps struggling to find a Muslim marriage partner

---

1 Muḥammad ibn Aḥmad Ibn Jubayr, *Riḥlat Ibn Jubayr* (Beirut: Dār Ṣādir, 1964), 315–16. English translation by R. J. C. Broadhurst, *The Travels of Ibn Jubayr* (London: Cape, 1952), 360.

in a community that was being diminished and demoralized. Or, perhaps, she was experiencing strong social and cultural pressures to convert to Christianity or to marry a Christian man and thus leave the Muslim faith community.

Ibn Jubayr also explained that the family hoped that, if she were to find a safe and secure home in Granada (by that time the only Muslim polity left in al-Andalus), the rest of the family might be able to join her there after the Norman travel ban was lifted. Emigration, rather than immigration, was restricted in part because the Normans relied upon the agricultural labour and tax revenue brought in from their Muslim subjects (who paid a reversed and Latinized form of the *jizya*, which they called the *gesia*). Ibn Jubayr noted his shock at the willingness of this family to separate from each other for the possibility of the daughter's migration, and speculated that their plight as subjected minorities must truly have been difficult in order for them to envision such a possibility.

Ibn Jubayr related this story with a sense of awe, marvelling at the desperation it signalled within the Muslim community broadly and this family in particular. For not only was this idea being presented as the father's idea, but as that of the girl herself; she was clearly not being exiled by her father but was seeking a better life in a new place for herself and her family. Ibn Jubayr noted the piety of the girl who was so willing to endure separation from her family in order to live in a Muslim land. And, not only was this girl the eldest daughter of the family, she was also motherless, meaning that the rest of the family (including two younger brothers and one younger sister) depended upon her for many of the domestic and emotional tasks that would otherwise have been the mother's job. So extreme was the family's desire to escape from Christian Sicily, so dire their sense that remaining there would harm their family's prospects, that they were willing to part from each other across a vast sea in order to possibly secure a future in a Muslim-dominated land. Similar desires must have motivated many other migrants and would-be migrants, even though most of their stories are lost to us.

The key element in this young woman's story was the question of her marriage partner. Ibn Jubayr does not tell us whether any of the Granadan pilgrims in his group accepted the family's offer, and we do not know what became of her or her family. But we can imagine that for many women seeking to migrate, the context in which they would do so was their family—either their natal family or their marital one. The Sicilian girl, possibly like other potential migrant women, sought to move not with her husband but in order to attain one. And for young women like this Sicilian Muslim, marriage outside of the local community must have been perceived as the only way they would be able to migrate, given the travel ban and the increasingly difficult conditions for the island's native Muslim population.

The Geniza records and rabbinic responsa can help us locate Jewish women migrants, many of whom also moved in the context of marriage or in order to get married.[2] They also allow us to witness the effect of men's mobility (whether for migration or more temporary travel) on women's lives. For Jews living in both the Muslim and Christian worlds, travel for business, pilgrimage, study, and migration was a regular cause of difficulty and loneliness. Many Geniza letters mention the emotional pain experienced by women whose husbands had departed on long commercial trips and not returned for a long time. At times, these husbands were feared dead, and at other times such men were known to have taken up with a new woman in a faraway place. Some women demanded divorce papers before their husbands left, in case they did not return—otherwise, the woman would be left in a state of uncertainty and unable to remarry. One Geniza letter from a husband includes a request that his wife and child join him in Sicily, where he had been forced to resettle because shipwreck and warfare in the region had prevented his return to Egypt. If she refused to move, however, he was willing to grant her a divorce and to pay child support for their son (Baskin, 225).

---

2 Judith Baskin, "Mobility and Marriage in Two Medieval Jewish Societies," *Jewish History* 22 (2008): 223–43.

Similarly, some marriage contracts included clauses pro-hibiting the new husband from moving far away from his wife or taking the wife with him and separating her from her parents. Marriages were contracted by a woman's family, and many families were concerned about the possibility of migration or even temporary long-distance separation from their loved ones. Several rabbinic responsa issued in Christian Europe demonstrate the regularity with which this problem arose. Rabbi Meir of Rothenburg, a thirteenth-century German Talmudic scholar, poet, and commentator, issued a number of judgments about where a husband could force his wife to migrate to. His repeated conclusion was that a husband could make his wife migrate to a town or a location of the same size as her place of origin, but not to a significantly different environment or much larger city. Nor could he ask her to move "to another country"—a dictum that then required him to explicate the nature of "countries" in the context of medieval Europe, a place without clear state boundaries (Baskin, 234–35). Language emerged as the deciding factor—if the migration crossed linguistic boundaries, it was not one that a wife was obliged to undertake against her will.

Sometimes, however, the advantages of a particular union outweighed any concerns about migration removing daughters far from their natal families. For example, several prominent young women—the daughters of various community leaders in Cairo—were known to have been married to men from Tunisia, Morocco, Lebanon, and the Yemeni port of Aden. All of these were places where Jewish merchant communities were especially active, and we can imagine that such marriages fostered business connections between families that appeared profitable to the women's parents. Geniza letters record a number of marriages with foreigners who travelled to Egypt, in which the woman then migrated with her husband back to his place of origin.

Other marriages appear to have been contracted from the start over long distances and across linguistic and cultural boundaries. One group of Jewish captives who had been ransomed after capture by Mediterranean pirates included several married couples and a lone girl, who was presumably on her way to be married overseas. She may have been sailing under the protection of one of the couples onboard. Rarely would a girl or young woman travel alone, but we see here a case in which one was entrusted to the care of a non-family fellow traveller; perhaps she was migrating to join her new husband abroad. But these long-distance migrations away from their natal families often caused the women significant emotional pain and distress. Several letters mention women from the Arabic-Jewish world, who had been married into Greek-Jewish families, who felt alone and wished to return home. For instance, one woman named Maliha had been married in Byzantium. She wrote to her brothers back home in Egypt, expressing her loneliness and her wish that they would come to retrieve her (Baskin, 230–31). However, this practice of marrying daughters to faraway husbands appears to have been more common among Jews in the Arabic-speaking world; in Christian Europe, fewer families of means opted to allow their daughters to move far away for marriage, preferring to keep daughters close to their parents and extended families.

Other common reasons for migration include religious conversion and poverty, both of which come together in a story found in Geniza letters about a poor woman convert in Spain. Born into an elite Christian community, the woman converted to Judaism and married a rabbi. They were forced to flee the wrath of her family, who were opposed to the union and to her conversion. Although they sought safety through migration, they and their children were later subjected to violence in their new town. They were attacked, the woman's husband was killed, and their two oldest children were captured. This left the woman and an infant child destitute and reliant upon charity as she moved from town to town seeking to raise the funds to ransom her older children (Baskin, 228). Letters from Jewish community leaders seeking support for this widow attest to her plight and give us a glimpse into the struggles she faced as a woman who had both converted and migrated before losing her family to violence.

Women and children were likely the most vulnerable immigrants, especially ones like this widow who lacked family support. But stories like that of the Sicilian young woman remind us that migration was rarely an individual event, even when our texts portray it that way. Most migrations involved wider communities or family groups. And like the mother in Sicily whose son migrated to Egypt, or like the many Jewish women whose husbands travelled far away, sometimes even when a woman herself was not an immigrant, she could be affected by its impact on her life and that of her community. Migration could be an agent of cultural transformation but also one of personal trauma.

Chapter 9

George of Antioch and Other Immigrants to Sicily

TWELFTH CENTURY

At the same time that Jewish and Muslim residents of Sicily were leaving, or seeking to leave, the Norman Christian island, the Latinate rulers were encouraging immigration of European Christians into their new realm. This typically meant settlement by knightly supporters of the Norman rulers, to whom they granted landed estates and who were attracted by the prospects of land and fortune in this formerly Muslim space. But the Normans also encouraged the migration of Western Christian church officials by establishing a number of Latin rite churches and monasteries. The Latin chroniclers who recorded the events of the Norman conquest and early decades of their rule were, for the most part, also immigrants to the island. Some came from nearby; the Normans likely drew many of their colonial settlers on the island from southern Italy. But others arrived from farther away, many of them from northern France (Normandy) like the Norman conquerors themselves. For example, one important chronicler of the period, Geoffrey Malaterra, claims that he himself came from "a region on the other side of the mountains, having only recently become an Apulian and indeed a Sicilian."[1] This may

---

[1] "Letter to Bishop Angerius," in Geoffrey of Malaterra, *De rebus gestis Rogerii Calabriae et Siciliae comitis et Robertis Guiscardi ducis fratris eius*, ed. Ernesto Pontieri, Rerum Italicarum Scriptores 2nd ser., vol. 5, pt. 1 (Bologna: Zanichelli, 1927–28). English translation by Kenneth Baxter Wolf, *The Deeds of Count Roger of Calabria and*

mean that he too was from Normandy, but in any event it is certain that he was an immigrant from the north who moved first to mainland Italy and then to Sicily.

Many people who took over estates, bureaucratic posts, and ecclesiastical positions in the process of "Latinizing" the island were Norman allies from Christian Europe—part of an intentional process of increasing the number of the Normans' loyal supporters on the island. But there does not seem to have been, at least initially, an organized effort to transform the entire ecclesiastical landscape of the island. Geoffrey Malaterra tells us that Count Roger I waited until the majority of the island had been conquered (ca. 1090) before attending to the distribution of ecclesiastical lands in Sicily. He, "lest he seem ungrateful that such benefits had been conferred upon him," (that is, by the pope) began to build churches and appoint bishops and abbots for Latin monasteries, while also initially allowing Greek monastic communities to maintain their traditions. But he found "the church to be uncultivated, having just been rescued from the jaws of the unbelievers," and thus in serious need of new leadership.[2] This so-called discovery suited Roger's dual purposes of pleasing the pope and increasing his Latinate population.

The newly appointed Latin ecclesiastical leaders were either taken from among the immigrant Latin Christian population or were enticed to move there to assume high-ranking positions. The chronicler presents Roger's appointments of these Latin clerics as part of an organized pattern of staffing the island's foundations with fresh leadership. Malaterra notes, for instance, that the first bishop of the newly built cathedral in Agrigento was a man named Gerland, a native of Savoy. He likewise tells us that the new bishop of Mazara was Stephen from Rouen. In Syracuse, the bishop was to be another Roger, a cleric from Provence, who had previously

---

Sicily and of His Brother Duke Robert Guiscard (Ann Arbor: University of Michigan Press, 2005), 42.

2 Malaterra 4.7; trans. Wolf, 182–84.

served as deacon in Troina (near Enna, Sicily).[3] These French clerics, like the warriors and landlords who settled on captured Muslim and Greek estates, were part of the larger waves of Latin migration meant to colonize the formerly Muslim island.

The monastery of St. Eufemia in Calabria, southern Italy serves as another example of a new foundation populated by immigrants from Normandy and other Latin Christian regions of Europe. The monastery had been founded by Robert Guiscard for one Abbot Robert (Robert de Grandmesnil) from Normandy who, according to Orderic Vitalis, had come from the Norman monastery of St. Evroul along with eleven monks.[4] They migrated southward as exiles due to a conflict they had had with the Duke of Normandy, William II ("the Conqueror"), who charged Robert with saying unkind things about him in private. After a stay in Rome under the protection of Pope Alexander II (1061–73), this group of exiles moved to southern Italy. There they sought refuge with other Normans who had come to Italy. They were eventually granted the new foundation of St. Eufemia by the conqueror Robert Guiscard, who endowed the monastery with large estates. He also placed under Abbot Robert's authority two more monasteries, both of which were also headed by monks who were newcomers to the region. One, the restored house of the Holy Trinity at Venosa, was given to another of the monks exiled from St. Evroul along with Abbot Robert. The other, at Mileto, was placed under a man named Angerius as abbot. He had come originally from Brittany to serve as a monk at St. Eufemia but was later chosen by Count Roger to become the bishop of Catania, in Sicily, before moving to the mainland to take the abbacy.[5]

In these few anecdotes, then, we can trace some patterns for the migration of northerners to Sicily during the Norman period. One commonality is that many of the ecclesiastical

---

3 Malaterra 4.7; trans. Wolf, 182–84.

4 Orderic Vitalis, *Historiae ecclesiasticae*, ed. Auguste Le Prevost (Paris: Julium Renouard, 1835–55), 82–91 (bk. 3, chap. 2).

5 Malaterra 4.7; trans. Wolf, 182–84.

newcomers to Sicily migrated first to southern Italy and thence to Sicily (or vice versa)—engaging in the multi-stage migration that we have seen in other stories. Southern Italy was in some sense a proving ground for many of the ecclesiastical and military leaders in the region, who might then move further south into the newly Christian-dominated frontier region of Sicily. These immigrants also were not exclusively Normans, despite what historians have taken to calling this invasion and conquest. The majority of these immigrants appears to have arrived from what we today call France, but at the time would have been the various semi-independent regions of Provence, Normandy, Brittany, etc.

These stories also highlight various common reasons that individuals undertook to move south. In the case of Abbot Robert and his eleven monks, Orderic Vitalis tells us that they were in exile from a fraught political situation in Normandy. They sought a safe place in several locations in Italy before finding a place at St. Eufemia under Robert Guiscard's patronage. Many other migrants may likewise have been seeking a safer new life in a frontier land, or were simply attracted by the promises of land, patronage, position, or fortune held out by the conquerors in the south. In this way, Sicily and southern Italy may have seemed to some in northern Europe as a land of opportunity, at the same time that Robert and Roger were seeking Latins to help populate their new lands taken from Muslim hands.

As we have seen already, however, the Normans were not only interested in inviting Latin Christian Europeans to their island. Their vision of a Mediterranean island kingdom also included patronizing artists, artisans, and scholars from Greek- and Arabic-speaking regions around the Mediterranean Sea. Prominent among these were scholars like the geographer and cartographer al-Idrisi, who produced Arabic-language texts and maps meant to enhance the reputation of the Sicilian royal court. Al-Idrisi was patronized by the first king, Roger II (r. 1131–54), and this relationship seems to have set a pattern that was followed by most of the succeeding Norman kings until Frederick II (r. in Sicily 1198–1250).

Even while dispossessing Muslims and Greeks of their lands and religious buildings, the Norman rulers invited artisans, scholars, and artists to their island from Muslim lands on the other side of the Mediterranean.

In fact, Ibn Jubayr, the late twelfth-century Muslim pilgrim and visitor to the island, remarked with some surprise on the number of Muslims employed (or perhaps enslaved) by King William II (1166–89)—cooks, tailors, concubines, bodyguards, and more. He also observed that this Norman practice was not limited to local Muslims but also foreign ones: "He pays much attention to his (Muslim) physicians and astrologers, and also takes great care of them. He will even, when told that a physician or astrologer is passing through his land, order his detainment, and then provide him with means of living so that he will forget his native land. May God in His favour preserve the Muslims from this seduction."[6] Although Ibn Jubayr was impressed with the number of Muslims and Arabic-speakers at the royal court, he was also concerned that the Christian king was attempting to ensnare those intellectuals and courtiers who came to the island but might not be allowed to leave. He seems to have feared that the Normans had a larger agenda of entrapment and conversion of Muslims to Latin Christianity, similar to the fear expressed by Imam al-Mazari about travellers to the island.

But not every Muslim intellectual who stayed at the Sicilian royal court was a long-term immigrant to the island; many stayed only temporarily. One example of short-term movement to the island is the poet Ibn Qalaqis (1137–72). He was an itinerant scholar and author, born in Alexandria and educated in Cairo, but was known for travelling widely throughout the Islamicate world. One of his journeys took him to Christian Sicily in 1186, where he first worked under the patronage of a local Muslim community leader named Abu al-Qasim.[7] After that, he moved to Palermo and wrote poetry for King William II. After about a year and a half on the island,

---

6 Ibn Jubayr, *Riḥlat*, 298–99; Broadhurst, *Travels*, 341.

7 Ibn Khallikān, *Wafayāt*, 5:385–89.

composing Arabic poetry in praise of his patrons, he was able to freely leave on a ship bound for Egypt.

The Norman rulers of Sicily were interested in inviting into their realm artists and scholars who could bolster their royal image as "Mediterranean" kings who presided over a culturally rich and luxurious court. But the island also welcomed immigrants who worked to help the Normans develop their systems of governance. Such highly placed migrants, whether scholars, artisans, or administrators, worked to support the administration and the self-presentation of the Norman kings as powerful rulers of a multi-ethnic and expansive kingdom.

One of the most powerful of such royal advisors to King Roger II was a Greek immigrant known as George of Antioch. He came to be called "*amiratus amiratorum*," or "emir of emirs," as leader of Roger's naval forces; this, we are told, was one of the highest-ranking Sicilian officials below the king himself. The story of George's arrival in Sicily and ascent to such high position is illustrative both of migration patterns in the Mediterranean generally and of the central position that Sicily played in many of the transformations within the medieval Mediterranean of the eleventh and twelfth centuries.

We are fortunate to have as complete a biographical profile of George of Antioch as could be hoped for. The Arabic historian al-Maqrizi records a lengthy biography, many details of which are confirmed by other sources.[8] His and his family's travels confirm a number of patterns that we have already seen in Mediterranean migrations: their multiple acts of movement and migration resulted both from regime change and from personal conflicts, with either personal patrons or political leaders. And they moved around from place to place before finding a final home and a profitable career in which they used the skills that they had acquired.

Even though George's recorded story begins in Byzantine Constantinople, his family was associated with Antioch, Syria.

---

8 Jeremy Johns, *Arabic Administration in Norman Sicily: The Royal Dīwān* (Cambridge: Cambridge University Press, 2002), 80–90.

This was probably the family's place of origin, and George continued to be identified with that city throughout his life. We are told that he was educated in Antioch and "elsewhere in the Byzantine East." Knowledgeable in both Greek and Arabic language and literature and also in financial administration, George and his father Michael eventually came to work for the Byzantine Emperor Alexius I Comnenus (1081–1118) in Constantinople. Antioch, a formerly Byzantine city in the Levant, had come under Turkish Muslim (Saljuq) rule in 1084; it is likely that the family left the city at that time, seeking refuge first in other unspecified Greek cities in the East and then finally in Constantinople.

After some time spent working in the imperial administration, either George or someone in his family came to be the target of a formal complaint to the emperor. We do not know the nature of the accusation, but it must have been credible because it caused the whole family to lose their positions and their home. The emperor had the entire family, women and children included, brought before him and sentenced to exile overseas. Exile was a regular tactic used by the Byzantine emperors against their political enemies. Although we do not know who among George's family was accused, or what the complaint against them was, the choice of exile as punishment suggests that it was a serious allegation.

We are not told the place to which they were being exiled, but wherever it was, they never made it there: they were instead diverted to a new life in North Africa. The ship on which the family had been placed was intercepted by the fleet of emir Tamim ibn al-Muʿizz of Mahdia. When the ship arrived at the North African port, the captives were able to get a personal meeting with the emir, who was impressed with their array of skills. Various family members were given positions in the Zirid administration, and George himself was made governor of the nearby port city of Susa. However, after a time of service to the Muslim emir, once again political intrigue and personal complaints made life in Ifriqiya untenable for the family. George's younger brother Simon angered one of the emir's sons, named Yahya. Simon had been caught spying on Yahya and reporting on what he learned—to whom and about what, we are not told. When this act of betrayal was discovered, he had Simon strangled in his sleep.

When Yahya succeeded his father as emir in 1108, George feared for his position and his life. The family then sought refuge in nearby Norman Sicily. Requesting aid from the Sicilians, George asked for a warship to come and rescue him. For whatever reason, this call for aid from the Christians worked. When the ship arrived with an ambassador from Sicily to the new emir, George and his family secretly slipped on board. The clandestine operation succeeded, and George and his family were able to sail away before anyone noticed they were missing.

Upon arriving in Sicily, George once again impressed his new ruler with his skills and facility with many languages. He was given a high-ranking position in the Sicilian royal administration and within a few years had attained the position of vizier, the rank closest to that of the king. As a very powerful vizier, George shaped Roger's royal policy and image in significant ways. Modelling Roger's royal presentation on that of Muslim potentates—crafting his public persona as luxurious and exotic, and sponsoring laudatory biographies to be written about him—George gained more and more favour with the king until he was given all the greatest honours and titles possible, including that of "emir of emirs." He also commanded Roger's navy, conquering islands and cities along the North African coast and making forays into the islands of the Greek East in the 1140s.

Tracing a path from Byzantine Antioch to Constantinople, thence to Muslim North Africa and on to Norman Sicily, George and his family zigzagged across the Mediterranean from one power centre to another. His career began haltingly, with a few missteps and close encounters with danger before he found a permanent post serving the Sicilian king. He lived to the age of ninety and, when he died, was succeeded by his son Michael. Thus this family of migrants found their way from one conquered city, through positions at two different political capitals (Constantinople and Mahdia) before finding a home, glory, and status in a third, Palermo. They endured conquest, exile, piracy, intrigue, and secret flight, but came out on top. Many other migrants, with less opportunity and luck, might not have found such success at the end of their journeys.

Chapter 10

Moses Maimonides

TWELFTH-CENTURY SPAIN AND EGYPT

The emotional difficulties of migration are demonstrated by the story of one of the medieval Mediterranean's most famous migrants, Moses ben Maimon, commonly called Maimonides. He is known as the greatest Jewish philosopher and scholar of religious law from the medieval period, and is still revered today as one of Judaism's most important thinkers of all time. His writings include biblical commentaries, a systematization of Jewish law, philosophical texts, and advice letters to Jews around the Mediterranean world in response to questions of concern to them. He was revered in his lifetime as both the chief legal expert of his community and for Jews in many other lands. All of this impressive intellectual output, as well as his career as a medical doctor, was made possible because he found refuge in a new land after a long and difficult migration from the place of his birth. As a migrant, he had special insight into the traumas experienced by people living under oppressive regimes, which he brought to his scholarship and legal responsa. And his own experiences of those traumas shaped his answers to questions from Jews facing similar problems, leading him to recommend migration rather than enduring persecution.

Most likely born in 1138, Maimonides was a member of the vibrant Jewish community that had lived in Islamic Cordoba for centuries, until a new North African religio-political power conquered much of al-Andalus. In 1148, Cordoba fell to the Almohads (al-Muwaḥḥidūn: "those who proclaim the unity of God," or "the unifiers"), an Amazigh-led movement to purify Islam of what they perceived to be corrupting influences. Among those influences was counted the presence of non-Muslim minorities, who were traditionally offered protected status according to the broader Islamic legal tradition. The Almohads, in contrast, emphasized the need for conversion to Islam by the peninsula's Jews and Christians. This reversal of the policy of protection for religious minorities led many Christians and Jews to pursue one of three options: to resist forced conversion (many who chose this path were sentenced to death), to convert nominally but continue to practise their religion in secret, or to flee to safer places. Maimonides and his family appear to have taken both options two and three.

Maimonides and his family converted to Islam in appearance and most likely practised Judaism in secret, trying to escape the notice of religious authorities. His body of writings also betrays ample evidence that he studied Islamic scholarly texts while the family sought to maintain their lives and status within Almohad territory. For unknown reasons, the family initially chose to relocate southward, rather than moving north to Christian territory as did other Christians and Jews, many of whom sought refuge in the Christian Spanish kingdoms or across the Pyrenees in Provence. Many prominent Jewish scholars from Cordoba, such as the Kimhi family of biblical scholars and the Ibn Tibbon family of translators and philosophers fled northward, but Maimonides' family moved south. Migrating first to Seville, the local Almohad capital, and later to Fez, in Morocco, Maimonides and his mother, father, brother, and at least two sisters spent around two decades trying to re-establish their lives within Almohad territories before finally moving eastward.

Scholars do not know exactly why the family chose to move around within Almohad lands initially, but some of Maimonides' later writings suggest that it was a difficult time for them. We have little detail about the experiences that Maimonides and his family went through in Seville and North Africa, however. He certainly studied philosophy and medicine, and began writing his first great work, the *Commentary on the Mishneh*, which was completed in 1168. That the completion of this work took place soon after he found a final home in Egypt shows that he had been studying and writing even while in the midst of his long experience of migration.

The fact that he studied and wrote while in transit does not mean that the migration period was an easy one for him or his family. He later wrote about his youth as a time of intense persecution and oppression, not only for himself but for all contemporary Jews. His personal experiences led him to consider his present time to be one in which the entire community of Jews was being threatened with extinction. And this fear compelled him to commit to writing immense amounts of his scholarly, philosophical, and legal learning. In fact, Maimonides was so convinced that he was living in a time of historical crisis that he felt obligated to write down things that were not, according to Jewish tradition, meant to be divulged in writing but only via oral transmission. He was, in other words, concerned that the events of his lifetime threatened to destroy the entire traditional framework of Jewish scholarship and the study of biblical and legal interpretation. This meant not only events external to the Jewish community (such as regime change and forced conversions) but also forces acting inside the diasporic Jewish community to disintegrate the community and its commitment to learning from within.

After nearly twenty years of trying to maintain their lives and livelihoods in the unwelcoming Almohad territories of the western Mediterranean, Moses and his family gave up and headed east, first seeking to settle in Jerusalem. Little is known about why they did not find it a profitable place to live, but the Christian crusaders who controlled the city were notoriously unwelcoming to Jews. It may also have been the case that they found little opportunity to establish themselves in profitable jobs there. After what appears to be a short time in Jerusalem, they moved to the Cairo suburb of Fustat, which was home to the thriving Jewish community of the Geniza records.

Many of Egypt's Jews were involved in commercial trade in both the Mediterranean Sea and Indian Ocean. Maimonides' brother David joined this economic community as a travelling merchant, supporting the family and making it possible for Moses to focus on his studies. When David died during one mercantile trip in the Indian Ocean in 1177, Moses was plunged into grief and a depression that lasted, according to his own account, for many years.[1] He also at that time was forced to begin earning money, since the family's patriarch Maimon had died soon after the family's arrival in Egypt. It was at that time that Maimonides began to practise medicine, which he did until his death in 1204.

The Egyptian Jewish community was, like pre-Almohad Cordoba, closely integrated into the economic and political world of the dominant Islamic culture. Ruled until 1171 by the Fatimid Shi'a caliphal government, Egypt was the centre of thriving trade networks that extended in many directions and in which Jews were deeply involved. Politically, too, Jews were allowed to maintain a level of autonomous self-government, although always at the discretion of the Muslim government. Moses Maimonides himself became the head of the Jewish community soon after his arrival there, and was considered the chief Jewish legal authority both in Egypt and farther afield. He had been appointed the head of the Egyptian Jewish community under the Fatimid regime, but that caliphate was soon overthrown by the future conqueror of crusader Jerusalem, Saladin, and replaced by a dynasty of Saladin's relatives called the Ayyubids. Using the title "sultan," they answered at least nominally to the Sunni Abbasid caliphs in Baghdad. This regime change was followed by a change in leadership in the Jewish community too, although Jews remained a protected group under Ayyubid rule, as was traditional within most of the Islamicate world.

Although Maimonides lost his position as head of the Egyptian Jewish community, he continued to be the most

---

I *Letters of Maimonides*, ed. and trans. Leon Stitskin (New York: Yeshiva University Press, 1977), 73–74.

important legal authority for Jews from around the Islamicate world. As a writer of letters and issuer of legal responsa, he advised Jews on the full range of problems and concerns confronting them. He also wrote his great synthesis and systematization of Jewish law, the *Mishneh Torah*, between 1168–77, soon after settling in Egypt. But his life in Egypt, while safe from the religious persecution he experienced in the Muslim West, was not always simple and happy. The deaths of his father and brother impacted him emotionally and professionally. He also suffered from political rivalries within the Jewish community and intellectual conflicts with other rabbis. And his status as a refugee continued to shape his own sense of identity, inflecting his sense of self with a sadness born from the loss of a homeland. He referred to himself as "among the exiles from Jerusalem who are in Spain," long after having left Spain itself.[2] And he traced his ancestry back through Spain, continuing to refer to himself as "the Spaniard" even after thirty years of living in Egypt (Halbertal, 16).

Maimonides' experiences as a migrant also shaped his perspective on how Jews ought to respond to oppression from non-Jewish religious authorities. His answer, essentially, was that emigration was preferable to death. Responding to an earlier pronouncement by a Jewish judge that death was the only correct option for Jews asked to convert or die, Maimonides wrote, from Fez in 1164/65, what is known as the *Letter on Apostasy*.[3] In it, he stated that nominal conversion to Islam was simply a matter of words, rather than action, and that therefore this so-called conversion was a better path for Jews than accepting death at the hands of the oppressors.

But beyond the question of nominal conversion, Maimonides advocated for flight to safety. In his letter he strongly encouraged migration as by far the best option: "the crucial advice I wish to give to myself and to those I admire and to

---

2 Quoted in Moshe Halbertal, *Maimonides: Life and Thought* (Princeton: Princeton University Press, 2015), 16.

3 "Letter on Apostasy" (1164/65), in *Letters of Maimonides*, trans. Stitskin, 34–69.

those who seek my opinion is to leave those places of hostility and go to a location where one could fulfill the Law without compulsion and fear. We should even forsake our homes and children and all our possessions, for the Divine Law we inherited means more for the prudent than all ephemeral possessions" (Stitskin, 65). His advice may have been a model for later Jews who faced expulsion and pogroms. For example, Nachmanides, the representative of Jewish beliefs in the Barcelona Disputation of 1263, migrated in the wake of that event. Having ostensibly lost the debate, which was staged by the Christian King James I of Aragon, he fled in fear for his life. By 1267 he had settled in Jerusalem, where he lived for the three remaining years of his life. During that time he wrote longingly of his homeland and his sense of exile, much like Maimonides, Ibn Hamdis, and others whom we have discussed here.

The migrant's choice—that is, Maimonides' choice—was viewed as the preferable way to preserve one's soul and life. For him, this was better than the choice of the martyr to accept death instead of nominal conversion and flight. Indeed, adherence to biblical law, according to Maimonides, dictated that Jews migrate rather than stay in a place where they could not practise their religion fully. They ought "to make every effort, no matter at what peril, to leave a hostile, non-Jewish place where religious practices cannot be observed properly and move to a more favorable location" (Stitskin, 66). This advice mirrors that encapsulated in the Islamic legal "obligation to emigrate" and also describes the lived experiences of many of the Christian immigrants of the early Middle Ages. Whether because of matters of religion, language, finances, or personal safety, we see that many other people made a similar calculation that migration was a far better option than remaining in a homeland where they lacked religious or other personal freedoms.

Religious Converts

NINTH TO TWELFTH CENTURIES

In contrast to Maimonides and other migrants who moved in order to safeguard their religious, linguistic, or cultural traditions after a regime change, some others migrated because they personally had changed religions when their community had not. The European Middle Ages was a time when religious identity was a predominant part of public culture, and religion was often used as a homogenizing force, employed to exclude or marginalize members of the non-dominant culture. Conversion from one religion to another was not in any sense a rare event in the premodern world, but for the most part those conversions were linked to large-scale demographic changes after a territorial conquest by rulers of a different religion. And, unfortunately for historians, most of these population shifts from one religion to another are nearly invisible in the historical record.

For many among the masses of people who slowly, or even quite rapidly, changed religions after a major conquest event, we may assume that the goal of belonging to the dominant language and culture was as important to their decision-making process as was belief in the tenets of the faith. There were others, however, who changed religions in directions that challenged the dominant culture, presumably as an act of faith and defiance, but sometimes also as a result of marriage: typically, women would have been expected to convert upon marriage to a member of a different religious community, while men were not. This may have been the main fear of the family of the Sicilian Muslim girl—that she would marry a Christian man and thus be expected to leave the community of Islam. And sometimes a religious conversion could prove to be dangerous, as we have already seen in the case of the elite Spanish Christian woman who converted to Judaism and ended up destitute after her family was attacked, her rabbi husband killed, and her children abducted.

Much like that woman and her family—who fled her hometown because they feared violence from her family after her conversion and marriage—many converts migrated out of fear. They might fear the social repercussions of their choice, or fear for their lives. But others made the decision to migrate so that they could be closer to communities of the faithful in their new religion. It would have been difficult, if not impossible, to fully practise many of the ritual and communal aspects of medieval religion outside of a group context, with its sacred spaces, objects, texts, festivals, and spiritual leaders. This fact was one reason for the Islamic legal injunction against remaining in a territory that had converted from Islam to another religion—the "obligation to emigrate." It also featured in Maimonides' determination that Jews should leave a hostile place rather than face death: they should seek a place where they could practise their faith freely. Those who did not would miss out on many important rituals and customs. This would then impoverish their personal faith, degrade their community cohesion, and threaten their unique traditions with extinction. Similar difficulties were faced by new converts, who needed the community of the faithful to instruct them in their new religion. Thus conversion to a non-dominant religion was often closely connected to migration.

One of the earliest such migrants whom we know of in medieval Europe was named Bodo, a convert from Christianity to Judaism. He had been a high-ranking chaplain at the imperial court of the Carolingian Emperor Louis the Pious but, in 839, he converted to Judaism and moved across the Pyrenees to the land of Zaragoza, which was ruled by Muslims. The Carolingian authors who recorded Bodo's story were most interested in what they perceived as his apostasy, rather than in the migration event itself.[1] They expressed amazement and disgust that someone like him, who had been educated deeply in the texts and traditions of Christianity from childhood, could make such an unlikely alteration to his religion and identity. And for them, this was indeed a change of identity as much as it was a change in belief and place of residence. The annal in which his conversion is recorded describes him also transforming his body, clothing, and name (as was regular for converts, since names were important markers of one's religious culture or regional identity): he was circumcised, let his hair and beard grow, and took the name Eleazar. When he moved to Spain, he also abandoned his clerical celibacy and married a Jewish woman.

Bodo's move to Islamic-controlled Spain was in fact not his first migration. He was referred to as an Aleman, meaning that his birthplace was significantly to the east of the Carolingian centres of power. Where Bodo lived before moving to the Carolingian court (with its ceremonial centre at Aachen but also itinerant for much of each year) is unclear, but likely was a prominent monastery in what would later be known as East Francia. It was not at all unusual for scholars, poets, theologians, artists, and clerics to move either permanently or temporarily to the imperial court. The Carolingians, beginning with Charlemagne himself, were deeply interested in fostering scholarship in both biblical and classical arts. They attracted to their court the best and brightest Christian intellectuals from all around the Latinate world.

Among the most prominent of these scholars was Alcuin of York, who came to Aachen from the north of England in the early 780s along with several assistants who moved with him. Alcuin became the head of Charlemagne's palace school

---

1 *Annales Bertiniani*, ed. F. Grat (Paris: Klincksieck, 1964), 27–28. Translation in J. L. Nelson, *The Annals of St. Bertin* (Manchester: Manchester University Press, 1991), 42. See also Frank Riess, "From Aachen to Al-Andalus: The Journey of Deacon Bodo (823–76)," *Early Medieval Europe* 13, no. 2 (2005): 131–57.

and an important proponent of the intellectual reforms that characterize the "Carolingian Renaissance." Until 790, Alcuin worked as teacher to Charles and his children, advisor to the king, and author of poetry, theology, and grammatical and other scholarly treatises. Although his move was not permanent, Alcuin continued to exchange letters with Charlemagne, and his impact on the development of the Carolingian intellectual program was immeasurable. Bodo was thus just one of many learned men from around the Latin Christian world who migrated to the centre of power in order to further their theological and intellectual careers. He was notable, however, in being the rare Christian who willingly converted to Judaism and left the court as an immigrant to Islamic Spain.

Interestingly, Bodo's big move came just a year after he had obtained permission from the emperor and empress to take a pilgrimage to Rome. It may be the case that he was simply preparing for his flight and used the pilgrimage as an excuse to leave the court without notice, or it may be that he converted during the journey. The annalists recording his apostasy and departure do not inform us, and it is not clear whether he converted before or after his trip, nor whether he even went to Rome at all. It is possible that he simply left Francia and went to Zaragoza directly. What is clear is that long-distance travel gave Bodo the opportunity to migrate to a new land and a new identity. We have seen how often medieval migration was intermixed with travel for other reasons—business, education, pilgrimage, and career advancement. Bodo/Eleazar's conversion to Judaism may have been rare, but his decision to use a long trip as the opportunity to migrate to a more religiously-welcoming place fits many of the larger patterns of medieval migrants.

Another convert to Judaism is known as Obadiah the Proselyte, who had previously been called Johannes of Oppido.[2] Like Bodo, he had more than one migration event in his personal history. Sometime in the 1060s his father had migrated

---

2 A collection of information and links about Obadiah are found at: https://johannes-obadiah.org/introduction.html.

from Normandy to the Italian town of Oppido—one of many knightly families who moved south as part of the first wave of Norman settlement in southern Italy. This process would eventually lead to the Norman conquest of Sicily and southern Italy, which, as we have seen, spurred even further waves of colonization by Normans and Latin Europeans who migrated to settle in the formerly Byzantine and Muslim lands. Part of the first wave of this process, Johannes' father moved to southern Italy and married a local Greek woman named Maria. She gave birth to Johannes and his twin brother Rogerius circa 1075. While Rogerius became a knight, Johannes became a monk.

Sometime around 1102, Johannes converted to Judaism and left Italy. He may have been following in the footsteps of another local convert, Andreas the former archbishop of Bari. Johannes/Obadiah included Andreas' story in his auto-biographical account, which is preserved in the Cairo Geniza cache along with a few other documents by or about him.[3] It is difficult to confirm the story of Andreas' conversion through external sources, although Obadiah records the event as a significant episode in his own life and decision to convert.[4] According to his account, Andreas' conversion—like Bodo's, that of a high-ranking clergyman well educated in Christian texts and theology—caused shock and dismay among the local Italian community. It also resulted in violence toward the convert, causing him to move more than once. According to Obadiah, Andreas migrated to Constantinople first and

---

3 English translation in Norman Golb, "The Autograph Memoirs of Obadiah the Proselyte of Oppido Lucano, and the Epistle of Barukh b. Isaac of Aleppo," in *Convegno internazionale di Studi Giovanni— Obadiah da Oppido*, available online at https://oi.uchicago.edu/research/individual-scholarship/autograph-memoirs-obadiah-proselyte-oppido-lucano-and-epistle-barukh.

4 An attempt to determine who, if anyone, the real Andreas might have been is found in Joshua Prawer, "The Autobiography of Obadyah the Norman, a Convert to Judaism at the Time of the First Crusade," in *Studies in Medieval Jewish History and Literature*, ed. Isadore Twersky (Cambridge, MA: Harvard University Press, 1979), 111–34.

there he formalized his conversion to Judaism by circumcision. But then "he arose and fled for his life from before the uncircumcised seeking to slay him" (Golb, 2). Migrating in fear a second time, Andreas moved to Egypt, where there was a significant Jewish population. According to Obadiah, he lived there the rest of his life.

Similarly, it appears that Obadiah ended his life in Egypt, which led to his memoir being included in the Cairo Geniza collection. The preserved text breaks off after recounting his years of travel after leaving Italy and before departing for Egypt. In the intervening nearly twenty years, he moved around from one Jewish community to another in the region of Syria and Iraq (but apparently avoiding crusader-held territories, meaning in particular that he never visited Jerusalem). First he went to Aleppo, then to Damascus and Baghdad, both places where he resided in the synagogue and was supported by the Jews of the community. His memoir includes a reference to "tribulations" and violence he experienced in Baghdad, as well as persecutions of Jews carried out there by the Muslim authorities (Golb, 5).

After some years in Iraq, Obadiah travelled to the north of Palestine and ended up in Tyre just a few years before it was conquered by crusading forces in 1124. From Tyre, Obadiah intended to sail to Egypt where, presumably, he lived in Fustat with the Geniza community whose records are so invaluable for understanding medieval Mediterranean Jewish life. Thus we see that Obadiah himself, like many other migrants we have encountered, moved several times before finally finding a permanent home. And, like the other converts here, his migrations and movements were specifically connected to his change in religion, both due to the violence of those opposed to the decision and to the desire to live among members of his newly adopted religion.

Other converts took similar paths, even if they led in opposite directions within Europe. For instance, Petrus Alfonsi, a Jew who converted to Christianity as an adult, was born in Muslim-controlled Spain but migrated northward after his conversion. He went first to England and then to France.

In his case, as in many others, his migration was also closely connected to his intellectual work, which was also linked to his religious experiences. Similarly, another Spanish Jew who converted to Christianity is known as Pablo Christiani. After his conversion to Christianity and his participation in a public debate, called the Barcelona Disputation (1263), with the Jewish scholar Nachmanides, he left Spain and travelled as a Dominican missionary.

Religious conversion in the Middle Ages was so deeply connected to migration that little has been written, by either medieval or modern authors, about the moves of converts like Petrus and Pablo; it was simply taken for granted that a convert would leave a homeplace that had become hostile to them. These conversions and resultant migrations, rare though they may have been in the Middle Ages, highlight the recurring themes in the history of medieval migration stories: they were motivated by desires for personal safety, a profitable and productive career, and the opportunity to live among people of their same religion.

Conclusion

These few examples of medieval migrants and their stories represent many of the most common reasons that medieval people undertook the expensive, dangerous, and uncertain path of migration across the Mediterranean Sea. There were certainly other reasons why people may have done so, and surely more individuals and groups who migrated than we know about from surviving sources. Peasants, for example, who moved from rural villages to the newly revitalized urban centres helped fuel the growth of cities in the central Middle Ages. Likewise, itinerant artisans and other economic migrants were part of the building boom of the period. Some long-distance merchants who brought trade goods from far away over land and sea may have chosen to settle abroad and start new lives rather than returning home. And to be sure, the triumphant conquerors and settlers of new lands—crusaders, for example, who remained in the conquered territories of the Levant, or the Magyars who moved westward from the Eurasian steppe region to settle in present-day Hungary—were part of medieval population movements more broadly.

But the patterns of individual migration seem clear: most migrants crossed the Mediterranean because of fear for their safety or personal freedom in the wake of regime change or after falling into disfavour with local authorities. Many others moved to find a profitable place to live and work among co-religionists, to set up business or to marry someone from another locale. Migration over long distances, especially that undertaken as an individual or as a family group, was not easy and often resulted in feelings of alienation in the new land. It appears that medieval people, like modern migrants, typically only migrated when circumstances seemed dire enough to make it seem like the only option.

And far more numerous were the medieval people who travelled or relocated for reasons that we might not consider voluntary migration, including forced exile, enslavement, or abduction. While some such moves involved isolated individuals who were captured and sold into slavery—like St. Elias the Younger—many more were the groups who were forcibly relocated or simply exiled from their homelands. For the most part, these expulsions were based on a group's religious identity. The Muslims of thirteenth-century Sicily, for example, were relocated to a mainland Italian colony at Lucera by King Frederick II. After centuries, first of rule of the island and then of inhabitation as minorities, the Muslim population was completely wiped out by this event. However, Frederick, like the preceding Norman kings, continued to invite foreign Muslim scholars and artists to his royal court. The community at Lucera did not last long: in 1300 it was decimated by the forces Charles II, King of Naples, when most of the inhabitants either slaughtered or enslaved.

Similar were the expulsions of Jews whose communities were progressively dismantled throughout most of western Europe over the later medieval period. Entire communities of Jews were expelled from various Christian kingdoms between the twelfth to fourteenth centuries, and moved in vast numbers to places considered safer and more welcoming. Often they were later invited to return—for example to England and to France—but did so as much diminished and impoverished communities. The final expulsion in 1492 fundamentally reorganized Jewish settlements in Europe—the once-vibrant Jewish communities of Spain and Aragonese southern Italy were emptied, and large numbers of Jews moved eastward to Ottoman Constantinople or to the Kingdom of Poland, where they were welcomed.

Examples like these, of community-level expulsion and exile, illustrate the larger point that the Middle Ages was not free from mass migration events, some voluntary and others coerced. But even as well-known as some of these large-scale events are, it is good to keep in mind that many individuals and families, like the ones profiled here, chose the path of migration in their search for individual safety, freedom, and a profitable life and livelihood.

Further Reading

Major Works in Mediterranean Studies

Abulafia, David. *The Great Sea: A Human History of the Mediterranean*. Oxford: Oxford University Press, 2011.

Braudel, Fernand. *The Mediterranean and the Mediterranean World in the Age of Philip II*. Translated by Siân Reynolds. 2 vols. New York: Harper & Row, 1972.

Horden, Peregrine and Nicholas Purcell. *The Corrupting Sea: A Study of Mediterranean History*. London: Blackwell, 2000.

McCormick, Michael. *Origins of the European Economy: Communications and Commerce, A.D. 300-900*. Cambridge: Cambridge University Press, 2001.

Pirenne, Henri. *Mohammed and Charlemagne*. Translated by Bernard Miall. London: Allen & Unwin, 1939.

"aDNA" (Ancient DNA) within Archaeology and History

Margaryan, A. D. J. Lawson, M. Sikora et al. "Population Genomics of the Viking World." *Nature* 585 (2020): 390-96. https://doi.org/10.1038/s41586-020-2688-8.

> A study on Viking era aDNA that demonstrated considerable genetic and phenotypic diversity especially among southern Scandinavian populations.

https://genetichistory.ias.edu/

> A multi-displinary team led by Patrick Geary uses modern science to shed light on the Germanic migrations of the sixth century CE.

The Development of Essentializing and Racializing Categories in the Middle Ages

Heng, Geraldine. *The Invention of Race in the European Middle Ages.* Cambridge: Cambridge University Press, 2018.

Rajabzadeh, Shokoofeh. "The Depoliticized Saracen and Muslim Erasure," *Literature Compass 16:e12548 (2019), https://doi.org/10.1111/lic3.12548.*

Tolan, John V. *Saracens: Islam in the Medieval European Imagination* (Columbia University Press, 2002).

Studies on Hadrian and Theodore in England

Lapidge, Michael. "The School of Theodore and Hadrian." *Anglo-Saxon England* 15 (1986): 45–72.

——. ed. *Archbishop Theodore: Commemorative Studies on his Life and Influence.* Cambridge University Press, 1995.

Constantine the African

Glaze, Florence Eliza. "Salerno's Lombard Prince: Johannes 'Abbas de Curte' as Medical Practitioner." *Early Science and Medicine* 23 (2018): 177–216.

——. "Introduction: Constantine the African and the *Pantegni* in Context." In *Medicine at Monte Cassino: Constantine the African and the Oldest Manuscript of his Pantegni*, edited by Erik Kwakkel and Francis Newton, 1–29. Turnhout: Brepols, 2019.

Green, Monica H. "The *De Genecia* Attributed to Constantine the African." *Speculum* 62 (1987): 299–323.

——. "The Genesis of the Medical Works of Constantine the African and Their Circulation in the Long Twelfth Century." Oral Presentation at the International Medieval Congress Leeds, 2016, available at: https://www.academia.edu/19301415/.

—— and Brian Long. "Ego Constantinus africanus montis cassinensis monacus." At https://constantinusafricanus.com/2017/12/22/.

Newton, Francis. "Arabic Medicine and Other Arabic Cultural Influences in Southern Italy in the Time of Constantinus Africanus (saec. XI²)." In *Between Text & Patient: The Medical Enterprise in Medieval and Early Modern Europe*, edited by Florence Eliza Glaze and Brian K. Nance, 25–55. Florence: SISMEL Edizioni del Galluzzo, 2011.

The Cairo Geniza

Cohen, Mark. *Poverty and Charity in the Jewish Community of Medieval Egypt*. Princeton: Princeton University Press, 2005.

Goitein, S. D. *A Mediterranean Society: The Jewish Communities of the Arab World as Portrayed in the Documents of the Cairo Geniza*. 6 vols. Berkeley: University of California Press, 1967–93.

——. *Letters of Medieval Jewish Traders*. Princeton: Princeton University Press, 1973.

Goldberg, Jessica. *Trade and Institutions in the Medieval Mediterranean: The Geniza Merchants and Their Business World*. Cambridge: Cambridge University Press, 2012.

Hoffman, Adina and Peter Cole. *Sacred Trash: The Lost and Found World of the Cairo Geniza*. New York: Schocken, 2011.

Krakowski, Eve. *Coming of Age in Medieval Egypt: Female Adolescence, Jewish Law, and Ordinary Culture*. Princeton: Princeton University Press, 2017.

Trade and Traders in the Mediterranean and Beyond

Abulafia, David. *The Two Italies*. Cambridge: Cambridge University Press, 1977.

———. "Christian Merchants in the Almohad Cities." *Journal of Medieval Iberian Studies* 2, no. 2 (2010): 251–57.

Chaffee, John. *The Muslim Merchants of Premodern China: The History of a Maritime Asian Trade Diaspora, 750–1400*. Cambridge: Cambridge University Press, 2018.

Constable, Olivia Remie. *Housing the Stranger in the Mediterranean World*. Cambridge: Cambridge University Press, 2003.

Dursteler, Eric. *Venetians in Constantinople: Nation, Identity, and Coexistence in the Early Modern Mediterranean*. Baltimore: Johns Hopkins University Press, 2006.

Jacoby, David. "Venetian Commercial Expansion in the Eastern Mediterranean, 8th–11th centuries." In *Byzantine Trade, 4th–12th Centuries*, edited by Marlia Mango, 371–91. Aldershot: Ashgate, 2009.

The Legal Injunction that Muslims Emigrate from Conquered Lands

Abou El Fadl, Khaled. "Islamic Law and Muslim Minorities: The Juristic Discourse on Muslim Minorities from the Second/Eighth to the Eleventh/Seventeenth Centuries." *Islamic Law and Society* 1 (1994): 141–87.

Davis-Secord, Sarah. "Muslims in Norman Sicily: The Evidence of Imām al-Māzarī's *Fatwā*s." *Mediterranean Studies* 16 (2007): 46–66.

Masud, Muhammad Khalid. "The Obligation to Migrate: The Doctrine of *Hijra* in Islamic Law." In *Muslim Travellers: Pilgrimage, Migration, and the Religious Imagination*, edited by Dale Eickelman and James Piscatori, 29–49. Berkeley: University of California Press, 1990.

The People and Administration of Sicily and Southern Italy

Catlos, Brian A. *Muslims of Medieval Latin Christendom, c.1050–1614*. Cambridge: Cambridge University Press, 2014.

Davis-Secord, Sarah. "Bearers of Islam: Muslim Women between Assimilation and Resistance in Christian Sicily." In *Gender in the Premodern Mediterranean*, edited by Megan Moore, 63–95. Tempe: Arizona Center for Medieval and Renaissance Studies, 2019.

——. *Where Three Worlds Met: Sicily in the Early Medieval Mediterranean*. Ithaca: Cornell University Press, 2017.

Granara, William. *Narrating Muslim Sicily: War and Peace in the Medieval Mediterranean World*. London: Tauris, 2019.

——. "Sicilian Poets in Seville: Literary Affinities across Political Boundaries." In *A Sea of Languages: Rethinking the Arabic Role in Medieval Literary History*, edited by Suzanne Conklin Akbari and Karla Mallette, 199–216. Toronto: University of Toronto Press, 2013.

Johns, Jeremy. *Arabic Administration in Norman Sicily: The Royal Dīwān*. Cambridge: Cambridge University Press, 2002.

Loud, Graham. "Communities, Cultures and Conflict in Southern Italy, from the Byzantines to the Angevins." *al-Masāq* 28, no. 2 (2016): 132–52.

——. *The Latin Church in Norman Italy*. Cambridge: Cambridge University Press, 2007.

Metcalfe, Alex. *Muslims and Christians in Norman Sicily: Arabic-Speakers and the End of Islam*. Abingdon: Routledge, 2002.

——. *The Muslims of Medieval Italy*. Edinburgh: Edinburgh University Press, 2009.

Simonsohn, Shlomo. *The Jews in Sicily*. 18 vols. Vol. 1, *383–1300*. Leiden: Brill, 1997.

Taylor, Julie. *Muslims in Medieval Italy: The Colony at Lucera*. Lanham: Lexington, 2003.

Moses Maimonides, His Life and Works

Bennison, Amira and Maria Angeles Gallego, eds. "Religious Minorities under the Almohads." Special issue of *Journal of Medieval Iberian Studies* 2, no. 2 (2010).

Corcos, David. "The Nature of the Almohad Rulers' Treatment of the Jews," *Journal of Medieval Iberian Studies* 2, no. 2 (2010): 259–85.

Fierro, Maribel. "Conversion, Ancestry and Universal Religion: The Case of the Almohads in the Islamic West (sixth/twelfth–seventh/thirteenth centuries)." *Journal of Medieval Iberian Studies* 2, no. 2 (2010): 155–73.

Halbertal, Moshe. *Maimonides: Life and Thought*. Princeton: Princeton University Press, 2015.

Kraemer, Joel. *Maimonides*. New York: Doubleday, 2008.

Stroumsa, Sarah. *Maimonides in His World*. Princeton: Princeton University Press, 2011.

Conversion or Assimilation to Islam

Bulliet, Richard. *Conversion to Islam in the Medieval Period: An Essay in Quantitative History*. Cambridge, MA: Harvard University Press, 1979.

Harrison, Alwyn. "Behind the Curve: Bulliet and Conversion to Islam in al-Andalus Revisited." *Al-Masāq* 24, no. 1 (2012): 35–51.

Islam, Christianity, and Judaism on Interreligious Marriage

Brundage, James. "Intermarriage between Christians and Jews in Medieval Canon Law." *Jewish History* 3, no. 1 (1988): 25–40.

Nirenberg, David. "Love between Muslim and Jew in Medieval Spain: A Triangular Affair." In *Jews, Muslims, and Christians in and around the Crown of Aragon*, edited by Harvey J. Hames, 127–55. Leiden: Brill, 2004.

Spectorsky, Susan. "Women of the People of the Book: Inter-marriage in Early Fiqh Texts." In *Judaism and Islam: Boundaries, Communication, and Interaction*, edited by Benjamin H. Hary, John L. Hayes, and Fred Astren, 269–78. Leiden: Brill, 2000.

Yamani, Mai. "Cross-Cultural Marriage within Islam." In *Cross-Cultural Marriage: Identity and Choice*, edited by Rosemary Breger and Rosanna Hill, 153–69. London: Bloomsbury, 1998.